299.

T H E
Words You Should Know How to Spell

· · · · · · ·

Michelle Bevilacqua

D1206430

BOB ADAMS, INC.
Holbrook, Massachusetts

Published by Bob Adams, Inc.
260 Center Street, Holbrook, MA 02343

ISBN: 1-55850-280-7

Printed in the United States of America

A   B   C   D   E   F   G   H   I   J

Library of Congress Cataloging-in-Publication Data
Bevilacqua, Michelle.
    The words you should know how to spell : the 10,000 most
commonly misspelled words / Michelle Bevilacqua.
        p.   cm.
    ISBN 1-55850-280-7 : $5.95
    1. Spellers.
    PE1146.B44   1994
    428.1—dc20   93-47469
                                                        CIP

*This book is available at quantity discounts for bulk purchases.
For information, call 1-800-872-5627.*

Contents

Acknowledgments

My sincerest appreciation and gratitude go out to the many people who offered their services and suggestions to bring this book to completion, especially: Steven Graber, Tami Monahan, Erica Jorgensen, Susan Moffat, Chris Ciaschini, Elizabeth Maher and her Uncle Kent, and anyone else who happened into the "bowling alley." Thanks also to Brandon Toropov for getting down into the dictionary trenches with me, and Kate Layzer for her usual top-notch text job. Finally, extra special thanks to Dawn Costello for all her help and dedication.

Introduction

This book is a comprehensive, convenient, and authoritative source of the correct spellings of thousands of difficult or confusing words. Unlike a dictionary, it features no cumbersome definitions, but takes you to the word you need—in just seconds. In addition, *The Words You Should Know How to Spell* contains a special section offering easy reference for those hard-to-spell cities, states, countries, and, yes, even planets and stars.

Some of the words in this book may seem simple, others a bit more obscure. Our goal was to provide the reader with a source that would supply words used every day—and also be of use in term papers, reports, articles, essays, and other specialized projects. This is, in short, a book for anyone who writes.

(*Note:* This book features *primary* spellings; many words have common, correct variant spellings as well.)

The Words You Should Know How to Spell

aardvark
Aaron
aback
abacus
abalone
abandon
abate
abattoir
abbe
abbess
abbey
abbreviate
abbreviator
abdicate
abdomen
abduct
abductee
aberrant
aberration
abet
abettor
abeyance
abeyant
abhor
abhorred
abhorrence
à bientôt
ability
abject

abjuration
abjure
ablation
ablative
ablaut
ablaze
ably
abnormality
abode
abolition
abolitionism
A-bomb
abominable
abomination
aboriginal
aborigine
abortifacient
abortion
abortive
about-face
aboveboard
aboveground
abracadabra
abrasive
abreast
abridge
abridgment
abroach
abroad

abrogate
abrupt
abruption
abscess
abscind
abscissa
abscond
absence
absent
absentee
absenteeism
absent-minded
absinthe
absolute
absolutely
absolution
absolve
absorbefacient
absorbency
absorptance
absorption
abstain
abstemious
abstention
abstinence
abstraction
abstractive
abstruse
absurd
abundance
abundant
abuse
abuser
abusive
abut
abutment
abuttals

abutter
abysm
abysmal
abyss
academia
academically
academician
a capella
accede
accelerate
acceleration
accelerative
accelerator
accent
accentual
accentuate
accept
acceptable
acceptance
access
accessible
accession
accessorize
accessory
accident
accidentally
accident-prone
acclamation
acclimate
acclimation
accolade
accommodate
accommodation
accompaniment
accompanist
accompany
accomplice

accomplish
accord
accordion
accost
account
accountable
accountant
accouter
accouterments
accredit
accreditation
accretion
accrue
acculturation
accumulate
accuracy
accurate
accurately
accuse
accustom
ace
acerbic
acetaminophen
acetic acid
acetone
acetylene
ache
achieve
achievement
Achilles
acid
acidic
acidosis
acknowledge
acknowledgment
acme
acne

acolyte
acoustic
acquaint
acquaintance
acquiesce
acquiescence
acquire
acquisition
acquit
acquittal
acre
acreage
acre-foot
acrid
acrimonious
acrobat
acronym
acrophobia
acropolis
across
across-the-board
acrostic
acrylic
activity
activities
actor
actual
actually
acuity
acumen
acupuncture
acute
adage
adagio
adamant
adapt
adaptable

addict
additive
address
adduce
adenoid
adequate
adequately
adhere
adherent
ad hoc
ad hominem
adieu
ad infinitum
adios
adjacent
adjective
adjourn
adjudicate
adjunct
adjust
adjustable
adjuster
adjustment
adjutant
ad-lib
administration
administrator
admirable
admiral
admiralty
admissible
admission
admittance
admonishment
admonition
ad nauseum
ado

adobe
adolescence
adopt
adorable
adoration
adore
adrenaline
adult
adulthood
adumbrate
advance
advantage
advantageous
adventitious
adventure
advertise
advertisement
advice
advisable
advise
adviser
advisory
advocate
Aegean
aegis
aerate
aerator
aerial
aerobics
aerodynamic
aeronaut
aeronautical
aerosol
aerospace
Aesop
aesthete
aesthetic

aesthetically
aesthetician
affable
affair
affect
affectionate
affidavit
affiliate
affinity
affirm
affix
afflict
affluence
affluent
afford
affront
afghan
aficionado
aforementioned
aforesaid
afraid
Africa
afterbirth
afterburner
aftereffect
afterglow
afterlife
aftermath
afternoon
aftershave
aftertaste
afterthought
afterward
against
agape
agate
ageism

agelong
agencies
agenda
age-old
aggrandize
aggravate
aggregate
aggressive
aggrieve
aggrieved
aghast
agile
aging
agitate
aglimmer
agoraphobia
agoraphobic
agrarian
agree
agreeable
agreeing
agricultural
agriculture
agronomy
aground
ague
aide-de-camp
aides
airborne
air-condition
airbrush
aircraft
airdrome
airdrop
Airedale
airfield
airiness

airlift
airline
airmail
airplane
airwaves
airy
aisle
ajar
akin
Alabamian
alabaster
à la carte
alacrity
Aladdin
à la king
à la mode
alas
albatross
albeit
albino
Albuquerque
alcohol
alcoholic
alcove
al dente
alert
algae
alias
alibi
alien
align
alike
alimentary
all-American
allege
allegiance
allegorical

allegory
allegretto
alleluia
allergenic
allergic
allergy
alleviate
alley
alleyway
alliance
allies
alligator
alliteration
alliterative
allopathy
allot
allotment
allotted
allotting
allow
allowance
alloy
all-purpose
all right
all-round
all-star
all-time
alluring
allusion
ally
almanac
almighty
almond
aloe
aloft
aloha
alone

aloof
aloud
alpaca
alpha
alphabet
alphabetize
alphanumeric
already
also-ran
altar
alter
altercation
alternate
although
altimeter
altissimo
altitude
alto
altogether
altruism
altruistic
aluminum
alumna
alumnae
alumni
alumnus
always
Alzheimer's disease
amalgam
amalgamate
amanuensis
amaryllis
amateur
ambassador
ambergris
ambiance
ambidextrous

ambiguity
ambiguous
ambitious
ambivalence
ambivalent
ambrosia
ambulance
ambulatory
ameliorate
amenable
amend
amendment
amenity
amenorrhea
Amerasian
American
amethyst
amiable
amicable
amid
amino
amity
ammonia
ammunition
amnesia
amnesiac
amniocentesis
amniotic sac
amoeba
among
amoral
amorous
amorphous
amortization
amortize
amount
amour

ampere
ampersand
amphetamine
amphibian
amphibious
amuck
amusement
anachronism
anachronistic
analgesic
analogous
analogue
analogy
analysis
analyst
analyze
anathema
anatomy
ancestor
ancestral
ancestry
anchor
anchorman
anchorwoman
anchovy
ancient
ancillary
andante
andiron
androgen
androgeny
androgynous
androgyny
android
andromeda
anecdote
anemia

anemometer
anemone
anesthesia
anesthesiologist
anesthetic
aneurysm
anew
angel
angle
anglicize
angora
angst
animalcule
animosity
anise
anisette
ankh
ankle
anklebone
annals
annex
annihilate
anniversary
anno Domini
annotate
announcement
annoy
annoyance
annual
annually
annuity
annul
annulled
annunciation
anoint
anomalous
anomaly

anomie

anonymity

anonymous

anorexia

anorexia nervosa

another

answer

answered

antacid

antagonist

Antarctic

Antarctica

ante-bellum

antecedent

antediluvian

antemeridian

antenna

antennae

anther

anthrax

anthropocentric

anthropoid

anthropologist

anthropology

anthropomorphic

anti-American

antibiotic

antibody

anticipate

anticipation

anticlimactic

antidote

antihistamine

antique

antisocial

antithesis

antonym

anxiety

anxious

anyone

anytime

anywhere

aorta

Apaches

apart

apartheid

apartment

aperitif

aperture

apex

aphasia

aphid

aphorism

aphrodisiac

Aphrodite

apiary

apiece

aplomb

apocalypse

apocalyptic

apocryphal

apogee

Apollo

apologetically

apologies

apology

apoplectic

apoplexy

apostasy

apostate

apostle

apostolic

apostrophe

apothecary

apothegm
apotheosis
Appalachian
appalled
apparatus
apparel
apparent
apparently
apparition
appeal
appear
appearance
appease
appellate
appellation
appendectomy
appendicitis
appendix
appetite
appetizer
applaud
applause
appliance
applicability
applicant
application
applies
appliqué
apply
appoint
appointee
apposite
appraisal
appraise
appreciable
appreciate
apprehend

apprehension
apprehensive
apprentice
apprise
approach
approbation
appropriate
appropriately
approval
approximate
apricot
a priori
apropos
aptitude
aquamarine
aquarium
Aquarius
aquatic
aqueduct
aqueous
arabesque
arachnid
arbiter
arbitrary
arbitration
arbitrator
arboreal
arboretum
arborvitae
arcane
archaeology
archaic
archdiocese
Archeozoic
archetype
archipelago
architect

archival
archives
Arctic
ardor
arduous
aren't
argot
arguable
arguing
argument
argyle
arid
Aries
aristocracy
aristocratic
Aristophanes
arithmetic
ark
Arkansas
armada
armadillo
Armageddon
armistice
armoire
aroma
aromatic
arouse
arpeggio
arraign
arraignment
arrange
arrangement
arrears
arrest
arrhythmia
arrival
arrive

arrogant
arrogate
arrow
arsenal
arsenic
arson
arterial
arteriosclerosis
artery
artfully
arthritis
arthroscopic
arthroscopy
artichoke
article
artificial
artillery
artistically
arugula
ascend
ascendancy
ascent
ascertain
ascertainable
ascetic
ascorbic
ascorbic acid
asexual
ashen
ashlar
ashore
Asia
asinine
asparagus
asperity
aspersion
asphalt

asphyxia
asphyxiate
asphyxiation
aspic
aspirant
aspiration
aspirin
assail
assailable
assassin
assassinate
assault
assay
assemblage
assent
assess
assessable
asset
assiduously
assign
assimilable
assimilate
Assisi
assist
assistance
assistant
associate
assonance
assort
assorted
assortment
assuage
assume
assure
asteroid
asthma
asthmatic

astigmatism
astronaut
astronomy
astute
asunder
asylum
asymptomatic
atavistic
atheist
atherosclerosis
athlete
athletic
athletics
atmosphere
atrocious
atrophy
attachable
attaché
attached
attachment
attain
attainable
attendance
attendant
attenuate
attire
attorney
attributable
atypical
auberge
auburn
au contraire
au courant
auction
audacious
audacity
audible

audience
auditorium
Audubon
auf Wiedersehen
auger
augment
au gratin
augur
August
Augustine
au jus
au lait
auld lang syne
au naturel
au pair
aural
aureole
au revoir
auricular
Auschwitz
auspice
auspices
auspicious
austere
authentic
author
authoritarian
authoritative
authority
authorization
authorize
autism
automatic
automatically
automation
automobile
autonomous

autumn
auxiliary
avail
availability
available
avalanche
avant-garde
avarice
avaricious
average
aversion
aviator
avid
avocado
avoidable
à votre santé
avuncular
awe
awful
awkward
awkwardly
axial
axiom
axis
axle
ayatollah
azalea
azimuth
Aztecs
azure
Babbitt
Babylon
baccalaureate
baccarat
bacchanalian
bachelor
bacillus

backbone
backlog
bacteria
bacterial
badge
badger
badminton
bagatelle
bagel
baggage
baguette
bailiff
bailiwick
baklava
balalaika
balance
balderdash
baleful
balk
ballad
ballerina
ballet
ballistics
balloon
ballot
balmy
baluster
balustrade
bamboozle
banal
banana
bandage
bandanna
bandeau
bane
bangle
banish

banister
banjo
banjos
bankruptcy
bannock
banquet
banqueter
bantam
baptism
baptize
barbarian
barbarous
barbecue
barber
barbiturate
bare
bargain
baring
baritone
barium
barley
bar mitzvah
barnacle
barometer
baron
baronet
baroque
barracks
barracuda
barrage
barrel
barren
barrette
barter
basalt
basically
basilica

basilisk
bas-relief
bass
bassinet
bassist
basso
bastard
baste
Bastille
bastion
bathe
bathhouse
bathing
bathos
batik
baton
battalion
batteries
bauble
bayonet
bayou
bazaar
beachhead
beacon
beady-eyed
beagle
béarnaise
bears
Beatitudes
beau
beau comp
beau geste
beauteous
beautician
beautiful
beauty
beaux

beaver
because
becoming
bedlam
Bedouin
bedraggled
beehive
Beethoven
beetle
befriend
befriended
beggar
beggary
beginner
beginning
begonia
behavior
behoove
beige
belfry
belie
belief
believe
believing
belle
belligerence
belligerent
benchmark
beneath
benefice
beneficial
beneficiary
benefit
benefited
benefiting
benevolent
benighted

benign
benzene
Beowulf
berate
beret
Bergen-Belsen
berserk
berth
besiege
besmirch
bespangled
bestial
bestow
bestowal
betray
betrothed
bettor
beveled
Beverly Hills
beware
bialy
biannual
biannually
bias
biased
bibelot
Bible
biceps
bicycle
biddy
bidet
biennial
bier
bigamous
bigamy
bigot
bijou

bikini
bilge
bilingual
bilious
billet
billet-doux
billiard
binary
binoculars
biography
biopsy
bipartisan
biped
birdie
biretta
biscotti
biscuit
bismuth
bisque
bistro
bitumen
bituminous
bivouac
bivouacked
bizarre
blab
blabbed
blabbermouth
blacklist
blamable
blanch
blancmange
blare
blasé
blasphemous
blasphemy
blatant

blazonry	bonanza
bleach	bonhomie
bleak	bonito
blessed	bon mot
blight	bonsai
blintzes	bonsoir
blithe	bon vivant
blitz	bon voyage
blitzkrieg	bookkeeper
blizzard	bookkeeping
bloc	boracic
blockade	Bordeaux
blotches	boreal
blouse	boric
bludgeon	boron
bluejacket	borough
bluff	borscht
bluing	borzoi
boatswain	bosky
bobbin	bossy
bobolink	Botticelli
boccie	botulism
bodacious	boudoir
Bodhisattva	bouffant
bodice	bouillabaisse
bogey	bouillon
bogus	boulevard
Bohemian	boundary
Boise	bounteous
boisterous	bountiful
bok choy	bouquet
boll weevil	bourbon
bolo	bourgeois
bologna	bourgeoisie
bomb	boutique
bombard	boutonniere
bona fide	bouzouki

bovine
bowdlerize
bowfin
boycott
Boy Scout
bracelet
braggadocio
braggart
Brahman
braid
Braille
braise
brake
brassiere
bravura
brawl
brazen
brazier
breadth
break
breakfast
breast
breathe
breathtaking
breed
breeze
brethren
bridal
bridge
bridging
brie
brief
briefly
brigadier
brilliant
brinkmanship
brioche

briquette
Britain
Britannica
Briton
brittle
broach
Broadway
brobdingnagian
broccoli
brochette
brochure
brogue
brokerage
bromine
bronchial
bronchitis
brontosaurus
bronze
brooch
broth
brouhaha
browse
bruise
brunet
brunette
brusque
buccaneer
bucolic
Buddha
Buddhism
budge
budgerigar
budget
buffalo
buffet
buffoon
buggies

bugle
bulbous
bulimia
bulldoze
bulletin
bullion
bulls
bully
bulrush
bulwark
bumblebee
bumptious
bundt
bungalow
bunion
buoy
buoyant
bureau
bureaucracy
bureaucrat
bureaucratic
burgeon
burglar
burglary
burgundy
burial
burlesque
burnout
bursar
buses
business
businesses
busing
bustle
butte
buttress
buxom

buzzard
bygone
bylaw
bypass
byte
Byzantine
cabal
cabala
cabalism
cabana
cabaret
cabbage
cable
caboose
cabriolet
cacciatore
cache
cachet
cacophonous
cacophony
cacti
cadence
cadet
Cadillac
cadmium
Caesar
caesura
cafe
cafe au lait
cafeteria
caffeine
cajole
calamari
calamitous
calamity
calcify
calcimine

calcium
calculable
calculus
calendar
caliber
calibrate
California
caliper
calisthenics
callous
callow
callus
calorie
calumnious
calumny
calypso
calzone
camaraderie
cambrian
cambric
camel
camellia
camera
camisole
camouflage
campaign
camphor
Canada
canal
canapé
cancel
canceled
canceling
cancellation
cancer
candidate
candle

candor
canine
canister
canker
cannabis
cannibal
cannoli
cannon
cannot
canoe
canopy
cantaloupe
cantankerous
canthus
cantilever
Cantonese
cantor
canvas
canvass
canyon
capable
capacious
capacitance
capacity
capillary
capital
capitulate
cappuccino
caprice
capricious
capricorn
capsule
captain
captious
carafe
caramel
carat

carat
carbohydrate
carbuncle
carburetor
carcinogen
cardiac
cardio-pulmonary
careen
career
carefree
careful
carelessness
caress
caret
caribbean
caribou
caricature
carnal
Carnegie Hall
carnival
carnivore
carnivorous
carotene
carouse
carousel
carpe diem
carriage
carried
carrot
carte blanche
cartel
cartilage
cartoon
cartridge
cascade
cashew
cashier

cashmere
casserole
cassette
cassock
castanets
caste
castigate
castle
casual
casualty
cataclysm
cataclysmic
catacomb
catalog
catalyst
catapult
cataract
catarrh
catastrophe
catatonic
Catch-22
category
caterpillar
catharsis
catheter
Catholic
catholic
Catholicism
caucus
cauliflower
caulk
causal
causation
cause célèbre
caustic
caution
cautionary

cautious
cavalcade
cavalier
cavalry
cavernous
caviar
cavil
cavort
cayenne
CD-ROM
cease
cedar
cede
cedilla
ceiling
ceilometer
celebrate
celebrity
celery
celestial
celibacy
celibate
cellar
cello
cellophane
cellulite
celluloid
cellulose
celsius
Celtic
cement
cemetery
Cenozoic
censer
censor
censorious
censure

census
centaur
centenarian
centenary
centennial
central
centrally
centrifugal
centripetal
century
ceramics
cereal
cerebellum
cerebral
cerebrum
ceremonious
ceremony
certain
certificate
cerulean
cervix
Cesarean section
cessation
cesura
cetology
Chablis
chafe
chaff
chagrin
chagrined
chain
chair
chaise lounge
chaise
chalet
chalk
challenge

chameleon
chamois
chamomile
champagne
champion
chancre
chandelier
changeable
changing
channel
channeled
chanteuse
chanticleer
Chanukah
chaos
chapeau
chaperon
chaplain
characterize
characters
charade
Chardonnay
charging
chariot
charismatic
charitable
charity
charlatan
charnel
chartreuse
chasm
Chassid
Chassidic
chassis
chaste
chastise
chateau

Chateaubriand
chatter
chauffeur
chauvinism
chauvinistic
cheap
cheat
checkup
cheddar
cheese
cheetah
chef
Chekhov
chemical
chemin de fer
chemise
chemist
chemotherapy
chenille
Cherokee
cherub
cherubim
chestnut
chevalier
Chevrolet
chevron
Chianti
chic
Chicago
chicanery
chickpea
chief
chieftain
chiffon
chiffonier
chignon
chihuahua

children
chimera
chimeric
chimney
chimpanzee
chinch
chinchilla
chintz
chintzy
Chippendale
chiropractor
chisel
chivalrous
chlamydia
chlorine
chloroform
chlorophyll
chocolate
choice
choir
choler
cholera
choleric
cholesterol
choose
chop suey
Chopin
chord
choreography
chorizo
chorus
chosen
chow mein
chrism
Christian
Christmas
chromatism

chromatography
chrome
chromium
chromosome
chronic
chronicle
chrysalis
chrysanthemum
chubby
chummy
churlish
chutney
chutzpah
cicada
Cicero
cider
cigar
cigarette
cilantro
cilia
cilium
Cimmerian
cinch
cinder
cinematic
cinematography
cinnamon
cinquain
cipher
circa
circle
circuit
circuitous
circular
circumambient
circumcise
circumcision

circumference
circumflex
circumlocution
circumspect
circumstance
cirrhosis
cirrostratus
cirrus
cistern
citadel
citation
cite
citify
citizen
citrus
civet
civil
civilian
civility
civilization
clairvoyance
clamber
clamor
clamorous
clandestine
clannish
claque
classic
classicism
classicist
classified
classify
clause
claustrophobia
clavichord
clavicle
clavier

clayey
cleanse
clearance
cleat
cleavage
cleaver
Cleopatra
clergy
clerical
cliché
client
clientele
cliff
climactic
climatic
climb
clinch
clinician
clipper
clique
clitoris
cloak
clock
cloisonné
cloister
cloistered
closet
closure
clothes
clothier
clown
clumsy
coach
coagulate
coalesce
coalition
coarsely

coattail
coaxial
cobalt
cocaine
coccyx
cochlea
cockamamie
cocktail
cocoa
coconut
cocoon
coda
codeine
codger
codicil
codify
coefficient
coequal
coerce
coercion
coercive
coeval
coexist
coexistence
coffee
coffer
coffin
cogent
cogitate
cogitation
cogito ergo sum
cognac
cognizance
cognizant
cognomen
cognoscenti
cohere

coherent
cohort
coif
coifed
coiffeur
coiffure
coincidence
coitus
colander
cole slaw
colic
colicky
coliseum
colitis
collaborate
collage
collapse
collapsible
collar
collared
collate
collateral
colleague
collect
collectible
collectibles
collector
college
collegial
collegiality
collegiate
collision
colloquial
cologne
colonel
colonize
colonnade

color
coloratura
colorize
colorless
colossal
colossus
colostomy
Columbia
column
columnar
columnist
comb
combated
combating
combustible
come-hither
come-on
comedian
comedic
comedy
comely
comer
comet
comfortable
comic
coming
comity
comma
command
commandant
comme ci comme ça
commemorate
commemoration
commemorative
commence
commendable
commensurate

commercial
commercially
commiserate
commission
commitment
committed
committee
commodious
commodity
common
commonwealth
communal
communicable
communicate
communications
communism
communist
community
commute
companion
companionable
comparable
comparative
comparison
compartmentalize
compass
compatible
compel
compelled
compensation
compete
competence
competent
competition
compile
complacent
complement

complementary
complete
complexion
compliance
compliant
complicate
complicity
compliment
complimentary
compose
composition
compote
comprehensible
comprehensive
compressed
compresses
comprise
compromise
comptroller
compulsory
computerized
comrade
concave
conceal
concealed
concede
conceit
conceited
conceivable
conceive
concentrate
concentric
concept
concert
concerted
concession
conch

conciliate
concise
conclave
concoct
concrete
concubine
concupiscent
concur
concurred
concurrent
concussion
condemn
condensation
condescend
condescension
condign
condition
conditioned
condor
conducive
conduct
conductivity
confabulate
confectionery
confederacy
confederate
conference
conferred
confess
confidante
confidence
confident
configuration
conflagration
confraternity
Confucius
congeal

congenial
congratulate
congratulations
congregation
congruous
coniferous
conjecture
conjoin
conjugate
conjunction
conjunctivitis
conjure
connect
connection
conniption
connive
conniving
connoisseur
connotation
connote
connubial
conquer
conqueror
consanguinity
conscience
conscientious
conscious
consciousness
consensus
consequence
consequently
conservation
conservatory
consider
considerable
consign
consignee

consignment
consistency
consistent
consolatory
console
consolidate
consommé
consonant
consonnance
conspicuous
conspiracy
constable
constant
constellation
consternation
constipate
constituency
constituent
constrain
constraint
construe
consul
consummate
consumption
contagious
contamination
contemporaneous
contemporary
contemptible
contemptuous
contentious
continent
contingent
continual
continually
continue
continuing

continuity
continuous
continuum
contour
contraception
contraceptive
contractual
contrariwise
contravention
contretemps
contribute
control
controlled
controller
controversial
controvertible
contusion
conundrum
convalesce
convenience
conversion
convertible
convex
conveyer
conveyor
convocation
convolute
convoluted
convulse
coolly
cooperate
co-opt
coordination
coot
Copenhagen
coping
copious

copyright
copywriter
coquetry
coquette
coquettish
cordial
cordon bleu
corduroy
coriander
Corinthian
cornball
cornea
cornet
cornice
cornmeal
cornucopia
coronary
coronet
corporation
corporeal
corpulent
corpus delicti
corpuscle
correlate
correspond
correspondence
correspondent
corridor
corrigenda
corrigendum
corroborate
corrosion
corrosive
corrugated
corruptible
corsage
corvette

Cosa Nostra
cosign
cosmic
Cossack
coterie
cotillion
cough
council
counsel
counseled
counselor
countenance
counterclockwise
counterfeit
countervail
country
countryside
coup
coup de grace
coup d'état
coupe
couplet
coupon
courage
courageous
course
courteous
courtier
couscous
cousin
couture
covenant
coveted
covetous
coxcomb
coxswain
coyote

cozy
crackle
Cracow
cradle
crag
crease
creation
creature
credence
credential
credenza
credible
creditable
credulous
Creole
crepe
crescendo
crescent
crevasse
crevice
cringing
crises
criteria
criterion
criticize
critique
crochet
crocheted
crocheting
crocodiles
croissant
croquet
croquette
cross-reference
croupier
crouton
crucial

crucible
crucifixion
crucify
crudités
cruelly
cruelty
cruiser
cruller
crumb
crustacean
cryptic
crystal
crystallize
Cuba
cubism
cubist
cubit
cuckoo
cucumber
cudgel
cudgeled
cue
cuisine
culinary
culprit
culture
cum laude
cumin
cummerbund
cumulus
cuneiform
cunnilingus
cupboard
cupful
Cupid
cupidity
curio

curiosity
curious
curium
curmudgeon
currency
current
curriculum
curry
cursory
curtail
curtain
curtsy
curvaceous
cusp
custard
custody
customary
cutlass
cut-rate
cyan
cyanide
cycle
cyclic
cyclical
cyclist
cyclone
cyclops
cygnet
cylinder
cylindrical
cymbal
cynic
cynical
cynicism
cynosure
cyst
cystic fibrosis

cystitis
czar
Czech
Dachau
dachshund
dactyl
daffodil
daguerreotype
dahlia
daily
daiquiri
dairy
Dalai Lama
dally
dalmation
damnable
damned
dandelion
dandle
dangerous
Dante
daub
daughter
daunt
dauntless
dauphin
dawdle
daylight
dazzle
deacon
deadlock
deaf
dealt
dearth
debacle
debatable
debauch

debauchery
debonair
debris
debt
debug
debugging
debutante
decaffeinated
decanter
decapitate
decasyllabic
deceit
deceive
December
decentralize
decibel
decide
deciduous
decimal
decimate
decipher
decision
declaration
declarative
décolletage
decorate
decoupage
decree
decrepit
dedicate
deducible
deductible
deem
de-escalate
deface
de facto
defalcate

defeat
defecate
defendant
defense
defensible
defer
deference
deferred
defiance
deficiency
deficient
deficit
defied
defile
definable
definite
definitely
definition
definitive
defuse
defy
Degas
de Gaulle
degradation
dehydrate
deification
deify
deign
deity
déjà vu
Delaware
delectable
delegate
deleterious
deletion
delft
deliberate

delicacy
delicatessen
delicious
delinquency
delinquent
delirious
dell
deluge
deluxe
delve
demagogue
dementia praecox
demerit
demise
demitasse
democracy
demographic
demonstrable
demonstrate
demur
denial
denigrate
denizen
denouement
dense
dental
dentifrice
dentin
denude
deodorant
deoxyribonucleic acid
dependable
dependent
deplete
deplorable
depose
deposit

deposition
depot
depravation
deprecate
depreciate
depreciation
depressant
deprivation
depths
deputy
derailleur
deranged
derelict
deride
de rigueur
dermatological
dermatologist
dermis
derogatory
derrick
derring-do
derringer
descend
descendant
descent
describe
description
descry
desecrate
desegregate
desert
desertion
deserve
desiccate
designate
desirable
desirous

desolate
despair
desperate
despicable
despondency
despot
despotic
dessert
destructible
detach
detachment
detail
detain
detergent
deteriorate
determinable
determinism
deterrent
detestable
detour
detriment
deuce
devaluing
devastate
develop
development
deviate
device
devious
devise
devoid
devotion
devour
dexterity
dexterous
diabetes
diadem

diagnose
diagnosis
diagrammed
dialect
dialogue
dialysis
diamond
diaper
diaphanous
diaphragm
diarrhea
diary
diaspora
diatribe
dichotomy
dictionary
diddle
didn't
diesel
diet
dietary
dietitian
difference
differential
diffuse
digest
digestible
digestion
digitalis
Dijon
dilapidate
dilemma
dilettante
diligent
diluted
dimensions
diminish

diminutive
dinette
dining
dinosaur
diocesan
diocese
Dionysus
diorama
dioxide
diphtheria
diphthong
diploma
diptych
dire
directories
dirge
dirigible
disability
disappear
disappoint
disapprobation
disastrous
disburse
discern
discernible
disciple
discipline
discombobulate
disconsolate
discotheque
discourage
discourteous
discreet
discrepancy
discretion
discretionary
discriminate

discursive
disdain
disease
disguise
dishevel
disillusioned
disingenuous
disintegrate
disparage
dispassionate
dispatch
dispel
dispensary
disperse
disposable
dispossess
disputable
dispute
dissatisfied
dissension
dissipate
dissonance
dissonant
dissuade
distinct
distinctive
distinguish
distortion
distraught
distribute
distribution
distributor
diuretic
diurnal
divan
divers
diversify

diverticulitis
divest
divide
divining
divisible
divulge
DNA
doable
docile
doctor
Dr. Seuss
doctrinaire
documentary
doddering
doesn't
dogwood
doldrums
doleful
dollar
dolorous
dolphin
domain
domestically
domestication
domicile
dominant
dominatrix
domineer
dominion
don
Don Juan
donkeys
donnybrook
donor
Don Quixote
dopamine
dormant

dorsal
dosage
do-si-do
dossier
Dostoevsky
dotage
double-entendre
douche
doughnut
dour
douse
dowager
dower
downfall
downside
downstairs
dowry
dowse
dowser
doxology
dozen
draconian
dragon
dragoon
dramatically
drastically
dread
dreadlocks
dreadnought
dregs
dreidel
dresses
drivel
drizzle
dromedary
dross
drought

drudgery
dryly
dual
dubious
duchess
duchy
duct
dulcet
dulcimer
dum-dum
dumb
dumbbell
dumbfound
dumbstruck
dumbwaiter
dummkopf
dumpling
dungaree
dungeon
Dunkirk
duodenum
dupe
duplicative
duplicitous
duplicity
durability
durable
duress
dutiful
duvet
dwarf
dwarves
dwell
dwelling
dwindle
dye
dyeing

dyer
dynamic
dynastic
dynasty
dyslexia
dysmenorrhea
dyspepsia
dysphasia
dysphemism
eager
eagle
earnest
earth
earthquake
Easter
eatery
eau de toilette
eaves
ebb tide
ebonite
ebullience
ebullient
ebullition
eccentric
eccentricity
Ecclesiastes
ecclesiastical
echelon
eclair
éclat
eclectic
eclipse
econometrics
ecru
ecstasy
ecstatic
ectomorph

ectopic
Ecuador
ecumenical
ecumenicism
eczema
eddy
edge
edgewise
edible
edifice
editor
eel
eerie
e.g.
effect
effectively
effervescent
effete
efficacious
efficiency
efficient
effluvium
effrontery
effulgent
effusion
effusive
egregious
egress
Egypt
eiderdown
eight
eighteen
eighth
ejaculation
eke
elapse
El Dorado

electoral
electricity
electrocardiogram
electrolysis
electrolyte
elegant
elegiac
elegiacal
elegy
elementary
elephant
eleventh
elicit
elide
eligible
elision
elite
elixir
ell
ellipsis
ellipsoid
ellipsoidal
elliptical
elocution
elocutionary
eloquent
elucidate
elude
elusive
Elysian
emaciated
emanate
emasculate
emasculated
embarcadero
embargo
embarrass

embassy
embezzle
embitter
embolism
embrocate
embroider
embryo
emergency
emeritus
emigrant
emigrate
eminence
eminent
emir
emissary
emission
emitted
emollient
emolument
empanada
empathy
emperor
emphasis
emphasize
emphysema
empirical
empiricism
emulate
emulsifier
emulsion
enable
enabling
enamel
enamored
encamp
encapsulate
encapsulated

encephalitis
enchant
enchilada
enclave
enclose
enclosed
enclosing
enclosure
encomium
encore
encourage
encumbrance
encyclical
encyclopedia
endangered
endeavor
endive
endocrine
endocrinology
endogamous
endometriosis
endomorph
endorsement
endoskeleton
endurable
enfant terrible
enforced
engagement
en garde
engender
engineer
enhance
enigma
enjambment
en masse
enmity
ennoble

ennui
enormous
enough
enounce
en passant
enquire
enrapture
enroll
enrollee
enrollment
en route
ensanguine
ensconce
ensemble
ensign
ensue
entail
entente cordiale
enterprise
enthrall
enthusiasm
enthusiastic
entice
entomology
entourage
entrée
entrepreneurial
entrepreneur
entropy
entry-level
enunciate
enunciation
envelop
envelope
enviable
envious
environment

envisage
enzyme
Eocene
eon
epaulet
ephemeral
epic
epicanthus
epicene
epicenter
epicure
epicurean
epidermal
epidermis
epigram
epigraph
epilepsy
epilogue
episcopal
episiotomy
episodic
epistemological
epistemology
epistle
epistolary
epistolic
epitaph
epithet
epitome
e pluribus unum
epoch
epochal
eponym
eponymous
equable
equaled
equalizer

equally
equanimity
equation
equestrian
equidistant
equilateral
equilibrium
equine
equinox
equipment
equipped
equitable
equity
equivalent
equivocal
equivocate
erase
Erie
erogenous
Eros
errancy
errant
errata
erratic
erratum
erroneous
ersatz
erstwhile
erudite
erudition
erupt
erysipelas
escapee
escargot
escarole
eschew
Eskimo

esophagus
esoteric
espadrille
especially
espionage
esplanade
espouse
espresso
essence
essentially
estimable
estimate
estrogen
estrus
estuary
et al.
etc.
etcetera
etch
ethereal
ethnicity
ethnocentrism
ethnology
etiquette
étude
etymology
eucalyptus
Eucharist
eugenics
eulogy
eunuch
euphemism
euphonious
euphony
euphoric
European
evacuee

evangelical
eve
eventually
eventuate
everyone
evidence
evil
evilly
evince
eviscerate
evolutionary
ewe
ewer
exacerbate
exaggerate
exalt
exaltation
exasperate
ex cathedra
exceed
excel
excellence
excellent
excelsior
exceptionable
exceptionally
excerpt
excerpts
exchequer
excipients
excise
excitability
excitable
excitative
exclave
exclusive
excoriate

excoriation
excrement
excrescence
excrescent
excrete
excruciating
excursion
excusable
excuse
execrable
execute
executive
exercise
exert
exeunt
exfoliate
exhale
exhaust
exhibit
exhibition
exhibitionist
exhibitor
exhilarate
exhilarating
exhort
exiduous
exiguous
exile
existence
existential
existentialism
exocrine
exodus
exogenous
exonerate
exorbitant
exorcism

exoskeleton
exotic
expansive
expatriate
expediency
expedient
expedite
expeditious
expel
experience
expiration
explanation
expletive
explicable
explicit
ex post facto
expunge
expurgate
exquisite
extant
extemporaneous
extempore
extemporize
extinct
extol
extramural
extract
extractive
extracurricular
extradite
extradition
extraneous
extraordinary
extrapolate
extrasensory
extraterrestrial
extraterritorial

extravagant
extravaganza
extrinsic
extrusion
exuberance
exuberant
exude
exult
exurb
eyelet
fabric
fabricate
fabulist
fabulous
facade
facet
facetious
facial
facile
facilitate
facility
facsimile
factious
factitious
factor
factorial
factual
faculty
Fahrenheit
faille
fait accompli
fajita
fakir
falafel
falchion
fallacious
fallacy

fallible
Fallopian
fallow
falsetto
falsify
falter
familiar
famine
famulus
fantasy
farce
far-fetched
farina
farrago
fascinate
fascism
fastidious
fatal
fatalities
fatigue
fatiguing
fatuous
faucet
faun
fauna
Faust
Faustian
faux
faux pas
favorite
faze
feasible
featherweight
febrile
February
feces
fecund

fecundity
feign
feint
feisty
feldspar
felicitate
felicitation
felicitous
fellatio
felonious
felucca
feminine
femme fatale
femur
fennel
feral
ferment
fermi
ferocious
ferociously
ferocity
ferret
Ferris wheel
ferrite
ferrous
ferrule
fertilizer
fervent
fervid
festoon
fetal
fete
fetid
fetish
fetter
fettuccine
feud

feudal
feudalism
fiancé
fiancée
fiasco
fiat
fiber
fiberglass
fibrosis
fibrous
fibula
fictitious
fiduciary
fief
fiefdom
field
fiend
fiendish
fierce
fiercely
fiery
fife
fiftieth
filament
filet mignon
filial
filibuster
filigree
filing
Filipino
filleting
fillets
fillip
filmic
filmography
filthy
finagle

finale
finally
financial
financier
fin de siècle
finesse
finicky
finis
finite
fir
fireplace
fishhook
fission
fissure
fisticuffs
fjord
flabbergasted
flaccid
flagellate
flagitious
flagon
flair
flak
flambé
flambeau
flamboyant
flamenco
flamingo
flamingos
flammable
flan
flange
flare
flash-forward
flashback
flaunt
flax

flaxen
flea
fleur-de-lis
flexagon
flexible
flexor
flier
flimflam
flimsy
flippant
flirtatious
floe
Florentine
floret
florid
Florida
florist
flotilla
flotsam
flounce
flourish
flout
fluctuate
flue
fluency
fluent
fluid
fluorescence
fluorescent
fluoridation
fluoride
fob
focused
focusing
foe
foie gras
foil

foliage
follicle
foment
fondle
fondue
font
footnote
forage
foray
forbearance
forcible
forcing
forebears
foreboding
foreclosure
forefather
forefront
forego
forehead
foreign
foreigner
foreknowledge
foreman
foremost
foreordained
forerunner
foresee
foreshorten
foresight
forest
forfeit
forfeiture
forge
forgettable
forgetting
formaldehyde
formally

formerly
formidable
forsake
forsythia
forte
forthright
fortieth
fortissimo
fortuitous
forty
forum
forward
fossil
fossilize
foulard
founder
foundry
fountain
four-flusher
fourth
fowl
foyer
fracas
fractious
fragile
fragrance
frail
fratricide
fraudulent
fraught
fray
free-for-all
freight
frenetic
frenzy
frequency
fresco

frescoes	funereal
fret	fungi
fretful	fungible
Freud	fungicide
Freudian	fungo
friar	fungoes
fricassee	fungus
Friday	fur
friend	furbelow
friendliness	furbish
friendly	furious
frieze	furlough
frijoles	furor
frisson	furrier
frivolous	furtive
frolicked	fuselage
frontier	fusillade
frontiersman	fusion
frontispiece	futile
froufrou	futility
frowzy	futon
frozen	futurism
frugal	futz
fruit	gabardine
fuchsia	gadabout
fugue	gadfly
fulcrum	gadget
fulfill	Gaelic
fulfilled	gaiety
fulminate	gait
fulsome	gala
fumble	Galapagos
fume	gale
fumigate	gall
function	gallant
fundamental	galleon
funeral	galleria

Gallipoli
gallon
galore
galvanize
gambit
gamble
gamesome
gamin
gamma globulin
gamma ray
gammon
gamut
Ganges
gangrene
gantlet
garage
garbage
garbled
gargantuan
gargoyle
garlic
garment
garnet
garnish
garret
garrulous
gaseous
gasify
gasket
gasoline
gastropod
gauche
gaudy
gauge
gaunt
gauntlet
gauze

gazebo
gazelle
gazette
gazetteer
gazpacho
gefilte
Geiger
geisha
gelatin
gelatinous
Gemini
gemology
gendarme
gene
genealogist
genealogy
generic
Genesis
genetic
genetically
Genghis Khan
genial
genie
genius
genocide
genome
genre
genteel
gentile
gentleman
gently
gentrification
gentrify
gentry
genuine
genuinely
genus

geodesic
geographic
geographically
geological
geometry
geopolitics
Georgia
geranium
gerbil
geriatrics
germane
gerontocracy
gerontologist
gerontology
gerrymander
gerund
gestalt
Gestapo
gesticulate
Gesundheit
geyser
Ghandi
ghastly
gherkin
ghetto
ghoul
giant
giantess
gibber
Gibraltar
gig
gigantism
gigolo
gild
Gilgamesh
gimcrackery
gimmick

gingham
gingivitis
ginkgo
ginseng
giraffe
girder
girdle
Girl Scout
gist
gizzard
glacial
glacier
glamorous
glamour
glasnost
glaucoma
glazier
glean
glib
glimpse
glissade
glissando
glockenspiel
glorify
glorious
glossary
Gloucester
glower
glucose
gluey
glutton
gluttonous
glycerin
gnarl
gnarled
gnash
gnat

gnaw	gracious
gneiss	gradation
gnocchi	gradient
gnome	gradual
gnomon	graduation
gnosis	graffiti
Gnostic	graffito
gnu	grammar
goad	grammarian
goatee	grammatical
gobble	granddaughter
gofer	grandeur
gondola	grandiloquence
gondolier	grandiloquent
gonorrhea	grandiose
good-bye	granules
googol	graph
googolplex	graphite
gopher	grapple
Gorbachev	grateful
Gordian knot	gratis
gorgeous	gratuitous
gorilla	gratuity
gospel	gray
gossamer	Grecian
gossiped	Greco-Roman
gossiping	gregarious
gossipy	grenade
gothic	grenadine
gouge	grief
goulash	grievance
gourd	grieve
gourmand	grieving
gourmandize	grievous
gourmet	grille
government	grimace
governor	grip

grippe
grisly
grizzly
grocery
grope
grotesque
grovel
gruel
grueling
gruesome
guacamole
guarantee
guarantor
guard
guava
gubernatorial
guerrilla
guffaw
guidance
guild
guile
guileless
guillotine
Guinea
guinea pig
Guinevere
guise
guitar
gullible
gurgle
guru
guttural
guzzle
gymnasium
gynarchy
gynecology
gyp

gypsum
gypsy
gyrate
gyre
gyroscope
habeas corpus
haberdasher
haberdashery
habiliment
habilitate
habitable
habituate
hacienda
hackneyed
haddock
Hades
haggard
haggis
haggle
Hague, The
Haight-Ashbury
haiku
hairsbreadth
haj
halcyon
hale
halibut
hallelujah
Halley's comet
hallmark
hallow
hallowed
Halloween
hallowing
hallucinate
hallucination
hallucinatory

hallucinogen	harum-scarum
halo	harvest
halogen	hasenpfeffer
halos	hashish
halvah	Hasidic
halves	hassle
halyard	hateful
hamburger	haughty
hammertoe	haunch
hammock	haunt
Handel	hausfrau
handicap	haute couture
handkerchief	haute cuisine
handle	haven
hangar	having
Hanukkah	Hawaii
haphazard	Hawaiian
happily	Haydn
hara-kiri	hazard
harangue	hazardous
harass	hazel
harbinger	hazelnut
harbor	headache
hardscrabble	health
hardware	healthy
harebrained	hearsay
harem	hearse
haricot	hearth
Harlequin	heartily
harlot	heath
harmonious	heathen
harpies	heave
harpsichord	heavy
harpy	heavyweight
harridan	Hebraic
harried	heckle
harrowing	hectic

hectogram
hectoliter
hectometer
hedgehog
hedonist
heebie-jeebies
heed
heifer
height
Heimlich maneuver
heinous
heir
heiress
heirloom
helical
helicopter
helix
helmet
helter-skelter
hemisphere
hemoglobin
hemophile
hemophilia
hemophiliac
hemorrhage
hemorrhoid
henceforth
hepatitis
heptagon
heptagonal
heptameter
herald
herb
herbaceous
herbarium
herbicide
herbivore

herbivorous
herbs
Herculean
Hercules
hereditary
heredity
heresy
heretic
heretical
heritage
hermaphrodite
Hermes
hermetic
hermetically
hermitage
hernia
heroes
heroin
heroine
heron
herpes
herring
herringbone
hesitate
heterodox
heterogeneous
heterosexual
hexagon
hexagonal
hexameter
hiatus
hibachi
hibernation
hiccup
hiccuped
hiccuping
hickory

hideous
hierarchical
hierarchy
hieroglyphic
hieroglyphics
highbrow
highfalutin
highlight
high-speed
highway
hijack
hilarious
Himalayas
hindrance
hinged
hinging
hinterlands
hippie
Hippocratic
hippodrome
hippopotamus
hirsute
historiographer
histrionics
hit-and-miss
hit-and-run
hitchhike
hoarfrost
hobgoblin
hodgepodge
hogwash
hog-wild
hoist
hokey-pokey
holiday
holiness
holistic

Hollandaise
holocaust
hologram
homage
homely
homeopathy
homestead
homeward
homicide
homiletics
homily
homogeneous
homogenous
homonym
homonyms
homophobia
homosexual
honeydew
honeysuckle
honky
honky-tonk
honorable
honoree
hookah
hooligan
hoopla
Hoosier
hootch
hootchy-kootchy
hoping
horde
horizon
hormone
hornet
horoscope
horrendous
horrible

horrific
horrified
horrify
hors d'oeuvres
horses
horticulture
hosanna
hosiery
hospice
hospitable
hospital
hostage
hostile
hotel
hotheaded
Houdini
house organ
houses
housing
Houston
hovel
hubbub
huckleberry
hue
humane
humble
humid
humidifying
humiliate
humility
hummingbird
hummus
humor
humorous
humus
hunger
hungrily

hungry
hurdle
hurricane
husband
hussy
hustle
hybrid
hydra
hydrangea
hydraulic
hydraulically
hydrogen
hydrogenated
hydrophobia
hyena
hygiene
hygienic
hygrometer
hymen
hymn
hymnal
hyperbole
hypertension
hyphen
hypnosis
hypnotist
hypocrisy
hypocrite
hypodermic
hypoglycemia
hypothalamus
hypothermia
hypothesis
hysterectomy
hysteria
iamb
iambic

Iberian
ibex
ibid.
Ibsen
ibuprofen
Icarus
ice cream
ice-cream cone
iceberg
icebound
icebox
icehouse
Ichabod
I Ching
ichthyology
ichthyosaur
icicle
iconoclast
iconoclastic
Idaho
ideal
ideally
ideogram
ides
idiocy
idiom
idiosyncrasy
idiot
Idlewild
idolatrous
idolatry
idyllic
i.e.
igloo
igneous
ignoble
ignominious

ignominy
ignorant
iguana
ileostomy
Iliad
ilk
ill fame
ill will
ill-advised
ill-bred
ill-conceived
ill-considered
ill-defined
illegal
illegality
illegible
illegitimate
ill-equipped
ill-fated
ill-fitted
ill-gotten
ill-humor
illicit
illimitable
illiteracy
illiterate
ill-kempt
ill-mannered
ill-prepared
ill-suited
ill-tempered
illimitable
illuminable
illuminate
illusion
illusory
illustrate

illustration
illustrious
image
imaginable
imaginary
imagination
imagine
imbalance
imbecile
imbecilic
imbecility
imbibe
imbroglio
imbue
imitable
imitate
imitation
immaculate
immanent
immaterial
immature
immeasurable
immediacy
immediate
immediately
immemorial
immense
immensity
immerge
immerse
immersion
immigrant
immigrate
imminent
immittance
immobile
immoderate

immodest
immoral
immovable
immune
immunization
immunodeficiency
immunize
impair
impale
impalpable
impanel
impartial
impassable
impasse
impassion
impassioned
impeach
impeccable
impecunious
impedance
impede
impediment
impenetrable
impenetrability
imperial
imperiled
impertinence
impervious
impetuous
impetus
impiety
impious
implacable
implement
implicit
imply
impolite

impolitic
importance
importune
imposition
impossibility
impregnable
impresario
impressionism
impressionist
imprimatur
impromptu
improper
impropriety
improvisation
improvise
impugn
impulsively
impunity
impure
impurity
impute
inaccessibility
inaccessible
inadequacy
inadequate
inadvertent
inalienable
inane
inanimate
inanity
inappropriate
inapt
inaudible
inaugural
inaugurate
inauspicious
incalculable

incandescent
incantation
incapacitate
incarnate
incendiary
incessant
incest
incestuous
inchoate
incidentally
incinerate
incipient
incise
incisive
incisor
inclement
incognito
inconceivable
incongruous
inconsolable
inconsonant
inconspicuous
incontinence
inconvenience
incorrigible
incredible
incredibly
incredulous
increment
incriminate
incubation
incubus
indebted
indecorous
indefensible
indelible
independence

independent
Indian
Indianapolis
indicative
indices
indict
indictment
indifferent
indigence
indigent
indignant
indigo
indispensable
indistinguishable
individually
indoctrinate
induct
indulge
indulgence
indulgent
industrious
inebriant
inebriate
inebriated
ineffable
inefficacious
inert
inertia
inevitable
inexorable
inextricable
infallible
infancy
infatuate
infatuation
infection
infectious

infer
inference
infiltrate
infinite
infinitely
inflammable
inflammation
inflation
inflection
influence
influenza
infrared
infrasonic
infrastructure
infrequent
infuriate
infuse
ingenious
ingenue
ingenuous
ingot
ingrained
ingratiate
ingratiating
ingredient
ingress
inhabitant
inhale
inhaler
inherency
inherent
inherit
inhibit
in-house
inimitable
iniquity
initial

initiated
initiation
initiative
inlaid
inland
innards
innate
inner tube
in medias res
in memoriam
innocence
innocuous
innovation
innuendo
innumerable
innumerate
inoculate
inordinate
inordinately
inquire
inquisitive
inroad
insanity
insatiable
inscrutable
inseparable
insidious
insignia
insignificance
insignificancy
insinuate
insipid
insistent
insofar
insole
insolence
insoluble

insomnia
insomniac
insouciant
inspiration
install
installation
installed
instantaneous
instep
instigate
instilled
instinct
instinctively
institute
instrument
insubordination
insular
insulin
insurance
insure
insurgence
insurgency
insurmountable
insurrection
intangible
integer
integral
integrate
intellectual
intemperate
intention
intercede
intercession
intercollegiate
interfere
interference
interferon

intergalactic
interlinear
interlocutor
interloper
intermarriage
intermediate
interment
intermezzo
intermittent
interpolate
interpose
interpret
interpretation
interpreter
interregnum
interrogate
interrogative
interruption
intersperse
interstellar
interstice
interval
interview
intestate
intimate
intoxicate
intractable
intramural
intransigent
intransitive
intrauterine
intravenous
intricacy
intrigue
introduce
inundate
invalid

inveigh
inveigle
inverse
invert
invertebrate
invidious
inviolate
involute
iodine
ion
ionic
ionosphere
iota
irascible
iridescence
iridescent
iris
irksome
ironclad
ironic
ironside
irony
Iroquois
irrational
irreconcilable
irreducible
irrefutable
irregular
irrelevant
irreparable
irresistible
irresponsible
irrevocable
irrigate
irrigation
irritable
irruption

Ishmael	jaguar
Isis	jalapeno
Islam	jalopy
island	jambalaya
isle	janitor
isolate	January
isolated	Japanese
isometric	jardiniere
isosceles	jargon
isotope	jasmine
Israel	jaundice
issue	java
isthmus	javelin
Italian	Jaws of Life
italics	Jayhawk
itinerant	Jazz Age
itinerary	jealous
it's	jeer
its	Jehovah
itty-bitty	Jehovah's Witnesses
Ivanhoe	jejune
ivory	Jekyll
Jabberwocky	Jell-O
jabot	jelly
jackal	jellybean
jackanapes	jellyfish
jackass	jellyroll
jackknife	je ne sais quoi
jack-o'-lantern	jeopardize
jackpot	jeopardy
jackrabbit	jerkwater
Jacksonian	jersey
Jacobean	Jesuit
jacquard	jet-black
jaded	jet engine
jag	jet-propelled
jagged	jet set

jet stream
jetsam
jettison
jetty
jewelry
jewels
Jezebel
jihad
jilt
jim-dandy
jingo
jingoism
jingoistic
jitney
jittery
Job
jockstrap
jocose
jocularity
jodhpur
jonquil
jostle
journal
joust
jovial
jowl
joyous
jubilant
jubilate
jubilation
jubilee
Judaeo-Christian
Judaism
judge
judgment
judicial
judiciary

judicious
juggernaut
juice
jujitsu
jujube
julienne
juncture
jungle
junket
junta
Jurassic
jurisdiction
jurisprudence
justice
justify
juvenile
juxtapose
kabob
Kafka
Kahlua
kaleidoscope
kaleidoscopic
kangaroo
karate
karma
katydid
Kauai
kayak
kazoo
keel
keelhaul
keen
keeshond
kerchief
kernel
kerosene
ketchup

keynote
khaki
Khrushchev
kibbutz
kibitz
kibitzer
kidnap
kidnaped
kidney
kielbasa
Kierkegaard
Kilimanjaro
kiln
kilowatt
kilowatt-hour
kilter
kimono
kin
kindergarten
kindle
kindred
kinesthesia
kinesthetic
kinetic
kiosk
kismet
kith
kitsch
kitschy
Kiwanis
kiwi
kleptomania
Klieg light
klutz
knack
knackered
knapsack

knave
knead
knee
knee bend
kneecap
knee-deep
knee-high
knee jerk
kneepad
knee-socks
knell
knickerbockers
knickers
knickknack
knife
knit
knitted
knitwear
knob
knobby
knock
knock-down-drag-out
knock-knee
knockwurst
knoll
knotted
know
know-how
knowledge
knowledgeable
knuckle
knuckleball
koala
kodachrome
Kodiak
kohlrabi
komondor

kosher
kowtow
Kremlin
Kriss Kringle
krona
Ku Klux Klan
Kubla Khan
kudos
kumquat
kung fu
kvetch
Kwanzaa
kwashiorkor
Kyrie eleison
label
labeled
labia
labium
labor
laboratory
laborer
laborious
labrador retriever
labyrinth
labyrinthine
lacerated
laceration
lachrymose
lackadaisical
lackluster
lacquer
lacrosse
lactate
lactose
lactovegetarian
laden
ladies

ladle
Laetrile
Lafayette
lager
lagoon
laid
lair
laird
laissez faire
laity
lakefront
lakeshore
lakeside
lamb
lambaste
lame
lament
lamentable
lamina
laminate
lampoon
lamppost
lanai
Lancelot
landfill
landlocked
landmark
landmass
landowner
landscape
language
languid
languor
languorous
lanolin
lantern
lapel

lapse	laureate
lapsed	laurel
larcenous	lavatory
larceny	lavender
larder	lavish
largely	law-abiding
largess	lawful
lariat	lawless
larrigan	lawman
laryngitis	lax
larynx	laxative
lasagna	lay
lascivious	layaway
laser	layoff
laser beam	layout
lass	layover
lassitude	Lazarus
lasso	lazy Susan
last-ditch	lazybones
lasvicious	league
latent	leakage
lateral	lease
Latin	leash
latitude	leasing
latitudinous	leather
latke	leatherneck
latrine	leaven
lattice	leavening
laudable	lecher
lauded	lecherous
laughable	lechery
laughter	lectern
launder	ledger
launderette	leech
laundress	leek
Laundromat	leer
laundry	leery

leeward	Lenten
leeway	lentil
left-of-center	leonine
lefty	leopard
legacy	leopardess
legal	leper
legality	leprechaun
legalize	leprosy
legato	lesbian
legend	lesion
legendary	letdown
legendry	lethal
legerdemain	lethargic
legibility	lethargy
legible	lettered
legion	letterhead
legislate	lettuce
legislative	leucite
legislature	leukemia
legitimacy	levee
legitimate	level
legitimize	leveled
legume	leveler
lei	levelheaded
leisure	leviathan
leisureliness	levitate
leisurely	levitation
lemming	lewd
lemonade	lexicography
lendable	lhasa apso
length	liability
lengthwise	liable
lengthy	liaison
lenient	libation
Lenin	libel
lens	libelous
Lent	liberal

liberalize
libertine
libidinous
libido
Libra
librarian
library
libretto
license
licentious
licorice
lie
liege
lien
lieu
lieutenancy
lieutenant
lifeguard
lifelike
lifeline
lifesaver
ligament
ligature
light
likable
likelihood
likely
lilac
lily
lima
limb
limit
limited
limn
limousine
limpid
linchpin

Lincoln
lineage
linear
lingerie
linguica
linguine
linguist
linguistic
linoleum
lionize
lip-sync
liquefied
liquefy
liqueur
liquid
liquidate
liquor
lissome
listen
literacy
literal-minded
literature
lithe
lithium
liturgical
livelihood
lively
lizard
llama
loaf
loafer
loath
loathsome
lobotomy
lobster
locale
localize

locally
loch
lodestone
logarithm
lollapalooza
loneliness
lonely
longevity
longitude
loose-leaf
lope
loquacious
lore
lorgnette
lose
losing
Lothario
Louisiana
Louisville
lounge
lousy
louver
Louvre
lovable
lovely
low-grade
lowbrow
lozenge
lubricate
lucid
lucre
ludicrous
luff
luge
luggage
lugubrious
lullaby

luminary
luminescence
luminescent
lummox
lunacy
lunatic
luncheon
luncheonette
lurid
luscious
lustrous
luxuriant
luxurious
luxury
lying
lymph
Lyndon
lynx
lyre
lyric
lyrical
macabre
macadam
macadamia
macaroni
macaroon
machete
Machiavelli
Machiavellian
machinery
machismo
mackerel
mackintosh
macramé
madam
Madame
Madeira

mademoiselle
madras
maelstrom
maestro
Mafia
mafiosi
mafioso
magazine
maggot
magi
magic
magician
magistrate
magna cum laude
magnanimity
magnanimous
magnesium
magnet
magnificence
magnificent
magnitude
maharajah
mahogany
mai tai
maidenly
maintain
maintenance
maitre d'
maize
majestic
major
majority
making
malachite
maladroit
malady
malaise

malapropism
Malay
malediction
malevolence
malfeasance
malice
malicious
malign
malinger
malleability
malleable
Maltese
mambo
mammal
mammalian
mammary
mammogram
mammoth
manacle
manageable
manager
manatee
mandarin
mandate
mandatory
mandible
mandolin
maneuver
manganese
mange
manger
mangoes
Manhattan
mania
maniacal
manicotti
manicure

manifest	marriageable
manifesto	married
manifold	marrow
Manila	marry
mannequin	Marseilles
manner	marsupial
mansion	Martian
mantel	martini
mantelpiece	martyr
mantilla	marvelous
manual	marzipan
manufacture	masculine
manumission	masonry
manuscript	masque
many	masquerade
maple	massacre
mar	massage
maraschino	masseur
maraud	masseuse
marble	massive
marchioness	mastectomy
Mardi Gras	master
margarine	masticate
margin	masturbate
marginally	masturbation
marijuana	matador
marimba	material
marine	maternity
marionette	mathematics
maritime	matinee
market	matriarch
marmalade	matriarchy
marquee	matricide
marquis	matriculate
marquise	matrimony
marred	matrix
marriage	matronly

matte
matter
mattress
maturation
mature
matzo
maudlin
Maui
maunder
mausoleum
mauve
maverick
maxilla
maximum
maybe
mayonnaise
mea culpa
mead
meadow
meager
meander
meanness
meant
measles
measure
measurements
mechanic
mechanical
mechanize
medal
medallion
meddle
Medicare
medicine
medieval
mediocre
Mediterranean

medium
medley
megalomania
melancholy
mélange
melanin
melanoma
mellifluous
mellow
melodious
melodrama
melon
membrane
memento
mementos
memoir
memorabilia
memorable
memorial
memory
menace
menacing
menagerie
menarche
menial
meniscus
menopausal
menorah
mensch
menses
menstrual
menstruate
menstruation
mental
mention
menu
Mephistopheles

Mephistophelean

mercantile

Mercator projection

Mercedes

mercenary

merchandise

mercurial

mercury

mercy

merely

meretricious

merger

meringue

merit

meritocracy

meritorious

merrily

mesmerize

Mesopotamia

Mesozoic

mesquite

messenger

Messiah

Messieurs

messy

metabolism

metabolize

metal

metallic

metallurgical

metallurgy

metamorphosis

metaphor

metaphysics

metastasis

meteor

meteorite

meteoroid

methinks

Methodist

meticulous

metropolitan

mettle

mezzanine

mezzo-soprano

Miami

miasma

mice

microfiche

microprocessor

microscope

midday

middle

middleweight

midriff

mien

migraine

migrate

Mikhail

mildew

mileage

milieu

military

militate

militia

millennium

milligrams

milliner

millinery

millionaire

milquetoast

mimic

mimicked

mince

mineral
mineralogy
minestrone
mingle
miniature
minimal
minimize
minimum
minister
minority
minotaur
minstrel
minus
minuscule
minute
minutia
minx
Miocene
miracle
miraculous
mirage
mire
mirror
misanthrope
misanthropy
miscegenation
miscellaneous
mischief
mischievous
misconduct
misconstrue
miscue
miser
miserable
miserly
misery
misfortune

mishap
misinterpret
mislaid
misogyny
missile
mission
Mississippi
Missouri
misspell
misstate
mistake
mistletoe
mistress
misused
mitten
mnemonic
moan
moat
mobilize
moccasin
mockery
model
modeled
modern
modest
modifier
modulate
modus operandi
modus vivendi
mohair
Mohammed
Mohammedan
Mohican
moiré
moiety
moisture
molasses

molecule
molestation
mollify
Molotov cocktail
molt
molten
momentous
mon ami
monarch
monarchy
monastery
Monet
money
moneyed
mongoose
moniker
monkey
monogamist
monogamous
monogamy
monogrammed
monologue
mononucleosis
monophonic
monopoly
monosyllabic
monosyllable
monotone
monotonous
Monsieur
Monsignor
monstrous
Montana
Montessori method
month
moor
mope

morality
morass
mordant
morgue
Mormon
Morocco
morphine
morsel
mortally
mortgage
mortify
mortuary
mosaic
Moses
mosque
mosquito
mossy
mother-of-pearl
motif
motion
motor
mottled
mountainous
mountebank
mournful
mousse
movable
movement
Mozambique
Mozart
mozzarella
Muammar
mucous (adjective)
mucus (noun)
muddy
mulatto
mulish

mullein
multicultural
multifarious
multinational
multiple sclerosis
multiply
mundane
munitions
murderer
murderous
murmur
muscle
muscular dystrophy
muse
museum
music
muslin
mussel
mustache
mustard
mutable
mutinous
mutiny
muzzle
myopia
myopic
myriad
myrrh
myrtle
mysterious
mystery
mystic
mystical
mysticism
mystify
mystique
myth

mythical
mythology
nadir
nagged
nail
naive
naiveté
naked
nameless
nanosecond
napery
Napoleon
narcissism
narcissistic
narcissus
narcolepsy
narcoleptic
narcosis
narcotics
Narragansett
narration
narrative
narrow
nascent
nastiness
nasturtium
natal
natatorium
national
nationalism
nationalistic
nationally
naturally
nature
Naugahyde
naughty
nausea

nauseate	neither
nauseous	nelson
nautical	nemesis
nautilus	neoclassicism
Navajo	neoclassicist
navy	nephew
Nazi	nepotism
Nazism	neptunium
near	nervous
neat	n'est-ce pas
Nebuchadnezzar	nestle
nebulous	nether
necessarily	neuralgia
necessary	neuritis
necessity	neurologist
neck	neurology
neckerchief	neuron
necromancy	neurosis
necrophilia	neurotic
nectar	neuter
nectarine	neutral
needle	neutralize
nefarious	nevertheless
negate	Newfoundland
negative	newsstand
neglect	next
negligee	nexus
negligence	niacin
negligent	Niagara
negligible	Niagara Falls
negotiate	nibble
negotiated	nicely
Negro	niche
Negroes	nickel
neigh	nicotine
neighbor	niece
neighborliness	Nietzsche

niggling
night
nightingale
nihilism
nil
nimble
nimbus
nine
nineteen
ninetieth
ninety
ninth
nipple
nirvana
nitrogen
nobleman
noblesse oblige
nocturnal
nocturne
noggin
noise
noisome
nolo contendre
nomad
nom de guerre
nom de plume
nominal
nominate
nominee
nonagenarian
nonagon
nonchalance
nonchalant
nondescript
nonentity
nonetheless
nonpareil

nonplused
non sequitur
noodle
normal
normalcy
normally
north
northerly
Norwegian
nosegay
nostalgia
nostalgic
nota bene
notable
notary
notch
notebook
nothing
notice
noticeable
notion
notoriety
notorious
Notre Dame
nougat
nourish
nouveau riche
nouvelle cuisine
novel
novice
novocaine
nowhere
noxious
nuance
nuclear
nucleus
nudity

nuisance
nullification
nullify
numb
numerous
numismatics
numskull
nunnery
nuptial
nurse
nursemaid
nurseries
nutrient
nutrition
nutritional
nutritious
nutty
nuzzle
nylon
nymph
Oahu
oar
oasis
oath
obdurate
obedience
obeisance
obelisk
obese
obey
obituary
object
objectionable
objective
object d'art
obligation
oblige

oblique
oblivious
obnoxious
obscene
obscure
obscured
obsequious
observance
obsession
obsolescence
obsolescent
obsolete
obstacle
obstetrician
obstinate
obstreperous
obtain
obtuse
obverse
obvious
occasion
occasional
occasionally
occupancy
occupant
occupied
occur
occurred
occurrence
ocean
oceanography
ocelot
ocher
octagon
octagonal
octane
octave

octogenarian
octopus
oculist
odd
ode
odious
odor
odorless
odorous
odyssey
Oedipus
offal
off-color
offense
office
official
officious
offset
off-the-record
often
oftentimes
ogle
ogre
ointment
Oklahoma
okra
old-fashioned
olfactory
olive
Olympic
omega
omelet
ominous
omission
omit
omnibus
omnidirectional

omniscient
omnivore
omnivorous
oncology
oneness
onerous
oneself
one-third
one-upmanship
ongoing
onion
onomatopoeia
onus
onward
onyx
opacity
opaque
openness
opera
operate
operatic
operator
operetta
ophthalmic
ophthalmologist
ophthalmology
opiate
opinion
opium
opponent
opportunity
oppose
opposite
oppressor
optic
optician
optimal

optimism
optomology
opulent
opus
oracle
oracular
oral
orange
orangutan
orator
oratorio
orchestra
orchid
ordain
ordinance
ordinary
ordnance
Ordovician
oregano
organization
organza
orgasm
orgiastic
orgy
Oriental
orientation
orifice
origami
original
oriole
ornament
ornamental
ornithology
orphan
orthodox
Orwellian
oscillate

oscillatory
osprey
ossify
ostensible
ostentatious
osteoporosis
ostrich
oubliette
ought
ounce
ours
ourselves
oust
outrageous
outweigh
ovarian
ovary
overall
overlook
overrate
overreach
overrun
overseas
overseer
overt
overture
overweight
overwrought
owl
oxygen
oxymoron
oyster
pachyderm
Pacific
pacifist
pacify
package

pact
padre
paean
pageant
pagoda
paid
painstaking
pair
paisley
pajamas
palatable
palate
palatial
Paleocene
Paleolithic
Paleozoic
palette
palindrome
palisade
palladium
pallid
palmistry
palomino
palpable
palpitate
palsy
paltry
pamphlet
panacea
panache
panda
pandemonium
pander
panegyric
paneled
panic
panicking

panicky
panjandrum
panorama
panoramic
pansy
pantomime
pantry
pantsuit
papacy
papal
paparazzi
paparazzo
papier-mâché
papilla
papillote
paprika
papyrus
parable
parabola
parachute
parade
paradigm
paradise
paradox
paraffin
paragon
paragraph
parakeet
parallel
paralysis
paralyze
paralyzed
paramecium
paramount
paramour
paranoia
parapet

paraphernalia
paraphrase
paraplegic
parasite
parasol
paratrooper
parcel
Parcheesi
pardonable
pare
parentheses
parenthesis
parfait
pariah
pari-mutuel
parish
parity
parlance
parliament
parliamentary
parlor
Parmesan
parochial
parody
parole
paroxysm
parquet
parrot
parse
parsimonious
parsley
parson
partake
partial
partially
participate
participle

particle
particular
particularly
parties
partisan
partition
partner
pas de deux
passable
passage
passé
passim
passion
passive
pastel
pasteurization
pasteurize
pastime
pastor
pastoral
pastrami
pastry
pâté
pâté de foie gras
patella
patent
paternal
pathos
patience
patient
patina
patio
patriarch
patriarchal
patriarchy
patricide
patriot

patriotism	penguin
patrol	penicillin
patron	peninsula
patsy	penitent
paucity	penitentiary
pauper	pennant
pavilion	penniless
peanut	Pennsylvania
pear	pension
peasant	pensive
pecan	pentagon
peccadillo	pentameter
peculiar	Pentecostal
pecuniary	penuche
pedagogue	penurious
pedal	penury
pedant	peon
pedestal	peonies
pedestrian	peony
pediatrician	people
pediatrics	pepperoni
pedigree	peptic
pedophile	perambulate
pedophilia	per annum
peer	percale
peerless	perceivable
peevish	perceive
Pegasus	percent
peignoir	percentage
Pekingese	percentile
pellucid	perceptible
penal	percolate
penchant	percolator
pencil	percussion
pendulous	peremptory
pendulum	perennial
penetrate	perforate

perfume
perfunctory
perhaps
perigee
peril
perilous
perimeter
period
peripheral
periscope
periwinkle
perjure
perjurer
perjury
perky
permanent
permeate
permissible
permit
permitted
pernicious
peroration
peroxide
perpendicular
perpetrate
perquisite
persecute
perseverance
persevere
Persian
persimmon
persistent
persnickety
personal
personnel
personification
perspective

perspicacious
perspiration
persuade
pertinent
perturb
peruse
pessimism
pesticides
pestle
petal
petit four
petite
petition
petrifaction
petrified
petrify
petroleum
petticoat
pettifoggery
petulant
pew
pewter
peyote
phaeton
phantasm
phantasmagoria
phantom
Pharaoh
pharmaceutical
pharmacopoeia
pharmacy
phase
Ph.D.
pheasant
phenobarbital
phenomenal
phenomenon

pheromone
phi beta kappa
philander
philanderer
philanthropy
philistine
philology
philosophy
philter
phlegm
phlegmatic
phobia
phobic
Phoenix
phonetic
phonics
phonograph
phony
phosphate
phosphorescence
phosphorus
photograph
photography
photon
phrase
phraseology
phyllo dough
physical
physically
physician
physics
physiognomy
physiology
physiotherapy
physique
pi
pianissimo

pianist
piano
pianoforte
piazza
pica
picayune
piccata
piccolo
picket
pickle
picnic
picnicked
pictorial
piece
piecemeal
pieces
pier
pierce
piercing
piety
piezoelectric
pigeon
pigment
pilaf
pilfer
pilgrim
pilgrimage
pillage
pillar
pillory
pimiento
pimientos
pimple
pina colada
pinafore
pinion
pinnacle

Pinocchio	platinum
pinochle	platitude
pinscher	platonic
pioneer	platoon
pious	platypus
pippin	plausible
piquant	playa
pique	playwright
piranha	playwriting
pirouette	plaza
Pisces	plea
pistachio	pleasant
pistil	pleasure
piston	plebeian
piteous	plebiscite
pithy	Pleistocene
pittance	plenary
pituitary	plenitude
pivot	plentiful
pixie	pleonasm
pizza	plethora
placard	pleurisy
placate	pliable
placebo	pliant
placenta	pliers
placid	Pliocene
plagiarism	plod
plague	pluck
plaid	plucky
plaintive	plumage
plait	plumber
planetarium	plume
plantain	Plutarch
plaque	plutocrat
plastic	plutonium
Plasticine	Plymouth
plateau	plywood

pneumatic
pneumatically
pneumonia
pocket
poem
poet
poet laureate
poetry
pogrom
poignant
poinsettia
poise
poison
poisonous
Polaris
polarize
Polaroid
polemic
polemicist
police
policy
polio
polite
politic
politick
politics
polka
pollen
polonaise
poltergeist
poltroon
polydipsia
polyester
polyethylene
polygamous
polygamy
polyglot

polygon
polygonal
polygraph
polymer
polysyllabic
polyunsaturated
pomade
pomegranate
Pomeranian
pompadour
pompous
ponderous
pongee
popsicle
popular
populous
porcelain
porcine
porcupine
pornography
porous
porpoise
porridge
portfolio
portico
portmanteau
portrait
Portugal
Portuguese
pose
Poseidon
posse
possess
possession
possible
postage
posterity

postern
posthumous
post-impressionism
post-modernism
postscript
postulate
potassium
potato
potatoes
potent
potential
potpourri
poultry
pour
poverty
practicable
practically
practice
practitioner
prairie
praline
prattle
preamble
Precambrian
precarious
precaution
precede
precedence
precept
preceptor
precinct
precious
precipice
precipitate
precipitous
precise
precision

preclude
precocious
precursor
predecessor
predestined
predicament
predicate
predictable
predilection
predominant
preeminent
preemptive
preen
preface
prefer
preferable
preferably
preference
preferment
preferred
prejudice
preliminary
prematurely
premier
premiere
premise
premium
preparation
prepare
preponderance
preponderant
preposterous
prerogative
Presbyterian
prescience
presence
preserve

prestige	probate
presume	procedure
presumption	proceed
presumptuous	process
pretense	procession
pretty	procrastinate
pretzel	prodigal
prevail	prodigious
prevalence	prodigy
prevalent	profane
previous	professional
prey	professor
prickly	proffer
priest	proficient
priestly	profligate
prima donna	profuse
prima facie	profusion
primary	progenitor
primer	progeny
primeval	progesterone
primitive	prognosis
primordial	programmable
principal	proletarian
principally	proletariat
principle	prologue
prior	Promethean
priorities	Prometheus
prioritize	prominent
priority	promiscuous
priory	promissory
pristine	pronounce
privet	pronounceable
privilege	pronunciation
prix fixe	proofread
pro forma	propagate
probable	propel
probably	propensity

property
prophecy
prophesy
prophet
propinquity
propitiate
propitious
proportional
proprietor
propriety
prosaic
prosciutto
proscribe
prosecute
proselytize
prosody
prospective
prosperous
prostate
protagonist
protégé'
protein
Protestant
Protestantism
protocol
proton
protract
proud
prove
providence
province
provincial
proximity
proxy
prurient
pry
psalm

pseudo
pseudonym
pseudonymous
psoriasis
psyche
psychiatrist
psychiatry
psychic
psychoanalysis
psychology
psychosis
psychotherapy
pterodactyl
ptomaine
publicize
pudgy
pueblo
puerile
Puerto Rico
pugilism
pugnacious
pulchritude
Pulitzer
pulley
pulverize
puma
pumice
pumpernickel
pumpkin
punctilio
punctilious
punctual
punctuate
puncture
pundit
pungent
puny

puree
purge
Purim
purlieus
pursue
purulent
purvey
purview
pusillanimous
putrefaction
putrefy
putrid
puzzle
Pygmalion
pygmy
pyorrhea
pyramid
pyromaniac
pyrotechnics
Pyrrhic
python
Qaddafi
quadrilateral
quadrille
quadriplegia
quadriplegic
quadruped
quaff
quahog
quail
qualify
quality
qualm
quandary
quantity
quarantine
quark

quarrel
quarreling
quarry
quartile
quartz
quasar
quasi
quatrain
quaver
quell
querulous
quesadilla
questionable
questionnaire
queue
quibble
quiche
quid pro quo
quiescent
quiet
quietude
quintessence
quintuple
quip
quirk
quisling
quixotic
quizzical
*quod erat
demonstrandum*
quorum
quota
quotidian
quotient
rabbi
rabbinical
rabble

rabies

raccoon

racial

racketeer

raconteur

radar

radial

radiate

radically

radiotherapy

radishes

radium

radii

radius

raiment

raisin

Raleigh

rally

ramble

rambunctious

ramekin

rampage

rampant

rancid

rancor

rancorous

rankle

ransom

rapacious

Raphael

rapier

rapport

rapprochement

rapt

rapturous

rarefied

rarefy

rarely

rarity

rasher

raspberry

ratable

ratatouille

rathskeller

ratio

rationalize

rationally

rattle

raucous

raunch

ravine

ravioli

raze

readily

reality

realize

really

rebellion

rebellious

recalcitrant

recapitulate

recede

receipt

receivable

receive

receiver

receptacle

recidivism

recipe

reciprocal

reciprocity

recognize

recollect

recommend

reconcilable	regency
recondite	regent
reconnaissance	regicide
reconnoiter	regime
recoup	regimen
recreational	region
recriminate	registrar
recrimination	registry
recruit	regression
rectal	regular
rectangle	regurgitate
rectify	rehabilitate
rectum	rehabilitating
recuperate	rehabilitation
recurrence	rehearsal
recycling	Reich
redden	reign
redemption	rein
reduce	reindeer
reducible	reinforce
redundancy	reiterate
redundant	rejoice
reenact	rejuvenate
reentry	relapse
refer	relay
referable	relegate
reference	relevant
referendum	reliability
referring	reliable
refrain	reliant
refrigeration	relics
refugee	relief
refulgent	relieve
refurbish	relieved
refutable	relieving
regale	religious
regatta	relinquish

reliquary

relish

reluctance

rely

remand

Rembrandt

remedial

remember

reminiscence

reminiscent

remiss

remit

remittance

remnant

remodeling

remonstrate

remotely

remove

remunerate

remuneration

remunerative

Renaissance man

renaissance

rendezvous

renegade

renege

renounce

renovating

renown

renunciation

repair

reparable

repartee

repast

repeal

repellent

repercussion

repertoire

repertory

repetition

repetitive

replete

replica

reply

repose

repossess

reprehensible

represent

representation

representative

repress

reprieve

reprisal

reprise

reprobate

reproduced

republic

reputation

reputedly

requiem

require

requisite

requite

requital

resalable

rescind

rescission

resemblance

reservoir

residence

residue

resilience

resiliency

resilient

resin
resistance
resistible
resolution
resonant
resounding
resource
respectable
respiration
respiratory
respite
responsible
restaurant
restaurateur
restoration
resume
resurrection
resuscitate
retaliate
reticence
reticent
reticulate
retinue
retort
retrieval
retrieve
retrograde
retrorocket
reveille
revelry
revenue
reverent
reverie
reversible
review
reviewer
Reykjavik

rhapsodic
rhapsodize
rhapsody
rhetoric
rheumatism
rheumatoid
rhinestone
rhinoceros
rhodium
rhododendron
rhubarb
rhyme
rhythm
rhythmic
ribald
riccotta
ricksha
ricochet
riddle
ridiculous
rife
riff
rifle
righteous
rigid
rigmarole
rigorous
riot
riotous
riposte
ripple
risqué
rite
rituals
ritzy
rivaled
rococo

Rodin
rogue
rollicking
romaine
rondeau
roofs
roommate
Roosevelt
Roquefort
Rorschach test
roseate
rosette
Rosh Hashanah
rote
rotisserie
rottweiler
rotunda
roué
rouge
rough
roulade
roulette
rousing
Rousseau
route
routine
roux
royally
rube
rubicund
rubric
rue
rueful
rumba
rumble
ruminate
rummage

rumor
rural
russet
Russia
rustic
rusticate
rustle
rutabaga
rye
Sabbath
sabotage
saboteur
saccharin
sachet
sacrament
sacred
sacrifice
sacrilege
sacrilegious
sacristy
sacrosanct
safari
safety
saffron
sage
Sagittarius
sahib
sake
salable
salacious
salami
salary
salient
Salk vaccine
sallow
sally
salon

salmon
salubrious
salud
saluki
Samaritan
Samoyed
sanctimonious
sanctuary
sanctum
sandwich
sangfroid
sangria
sanguine
sans
Sanskrit
sapphire
sarcastic
sarcophagus
sardonic
sarong
sarsaparilla
Saskatchewan
sassafras
satchel
satellite
satiate
satire
satirize
satori
satyrs
sauce
sauerkraut
sausage
sauté
Savannah
savior faire
savvy

sawdust
saxophone
scabies
scalene
scallions
scalloped
scallops
scampi
scandalous
Scandinavia
scanty
scapegoat
scarce
scarcely
scenario
scene
scenery
scenic
schedule
scheme
schism
schizophrenia
schlemiel
schlep
schlimazel
schmaltz
schmaltzy
schnapps
Schnauzer
scholar
scholastic
schrod
Schubert
science
scientist
scimitar
scintillate

scion
scissors
sclerosis
scone
scones
Scorpio
scorpion
Scripture
scrumptious
scruple
scrupulous
scrutable
scrutinize
scrutiny
scull
scurrilous
scythe
sea urchin
seance
Seattle
sebaceous
seborrhea
secede
secession
seclude
secretary
secrete
secularize
Seder
sediment
sedimentary
sedition
seditious
sedulous
seek
seethe
segregate

segue
seismic
seize
seizure
seltzer
semen
semester
Semite
Semitic
senile
senior
sensible
sensuous
sententious
separable
separate
sepia
September
septic
septuagenarian
septuagenary
sepulcher
sepulchral
sequel
sequential
sequester
sequestration
sequin
seraph
seraphim
serendipity
serf
sergeant
serial
series
seriocomic
serious

serpentine
serriform
serum
serviceable
sesame
sesquicentennial
sessile
settee
seventieth
several
Shakespeare
Shakespearean
shale
shallot
shanghai
Shangri-La
shantung
shanty
shaping
Shavian
sheathe
sheik
shellac
shellacked
shepherd
sherbet
sheriff
shield
Shih Tzu
shining
shipped
shipyard
shirred
shish kebob
Shogun
shoo-in
shook-up

shoot-out
shoptalk
shoreline
short-circuit
short-lived
shortsighted
shortstop
short-tempered
short-wave
shot-put
shotgun
shoulder
shovel
shoveled
showboat
showcase
showdown
showgirl
showman
showoff
showpiece
shriek
shun
shunt
shyster
Siamese
Siberia
siege
sienna
Sierra
siesta
sieve
signature
significant
silhouette
silicon
silicone

similar
simile
simulate
simultaneous
simultaneously
sincerely
sincerity
sine qua non
sinecure
singsong
sinistral
sinuous
sinus
Sisyphus
site
situation
sixtieth
skein
skeleton
skeptic
skeptical
skewered
ski
skied
skiing
skillful
skittish
skulk
skullduggery
slander
slanderous
slaughter
Slavic
sleigh
sleuth
sloe
sloe-eyed

slog
sloth
slovenly
slow-dance
sluggish
sluice
smarmy
smidgen
smoky
smolder
smorgasbord
smote
snafu
snapshot
snare
snit
snooze
so-and-so
sobriety
sobriquet
so-called
sociable
social
Social Security
socialist
societies
society
sociopath
Socrates
sodium
soften
software
soiree
sojourn
solace
solar
soldier

soldiering
soldierly
solely
solemn
solenoid
solicit
solicitous
soliloquize
soliloquy
solipsistic
solitaire
solstice
solution
somber
sombrero
sometime
sometimes
somnambulate
somnolent
sonata
sophism
sophisticated
sophistry
Sophocles
sophomore
sophomoric
soporific
soprano
sorcery
sordid
sorghum
soufflé
soupçon
sousaphone
southeast
southwest
souvenir

sovereign
sovereignty
soviet
spacious
spaghetti
spandex
Spaniard
spaniel
sparsely
spate
spay
special
specialized
specialty
species
specifically
specification
specified
specify
specimen
specious
spectacle
spectacular
speech
spew
sphere
sphinx
spiel
spinach
spindle
spirit
spiritual
spittoon
spondee
sponsor
spontaneity
spontaneous

spoonerism
sporadic
spouse
spry
spumoni
spurious
spurn
sputnik
squabbling
squall
squalor
squash
squeak
squirrel
stable
staccato
staid
stalactite
stalagmite
stalemate
stamen
stanchion
stanza
stasis
stationary
stationery
statistic
statuesque
statuette
status quo
stealthy
steeple
stegosaur
stein
stencil
stenciling
stentorian

steppe
sterile
sterility
sternum
stethoscope
stevedore
stigma
stiletto
stilted
stimulus
stipend
stoat
Stockholm
stoic
stoical
stoicism
stolid
stopgap
straddle
strafe
strafing
straight
straightway
strait
strait-laced
strangulate
stratagem
strategies
strategy
stratosphere
stratus
strenuous
strenuously
streusel
stria
strictly
stringent

stroganoff
strudel
strychnine
stubbornness
stucco
stuccoed
studious
stultify
stupefaction
stupefy
stupefying
stupor
sturgeon
style
stylus
stymie
styptic
Styrofoam
suave
subcutaneous
subdue
submitted
subpoena
subpoenaed
subpoenaing
subservient
subsidies
substantiate
substitute
subterfuge
subtle
subtlety
suburban
succeed
success
successful
successfully

succession
successive
succinct
succor
suede
suet
sufferer
sufficient
suffrage
suffragette
suggestive
suicide
suitable
suite
suitor
sulfur
sultry
sumac
summa cum laude
summarize
summary
summoned
sumptuous
sundae
supercilious
superfluous
superintendent
supersede
superstition
superstitious
supple
supplement
supplementary
suppliant
supplicate
supply
suppress

sure
surf
surfeit
surgeon
surging
surly
surmise
surprise
surreal
surrealist
surrealistic
surreptitious
surrogate
surveillance
susceptible
sushi
suspense
suspicion
suspicious
sustain
susurrant
svelte
Svengali
Swahili
swami
sward
swathe
Switzerland
swollen
sword
sybarite
sycamore
sycophant
syllable
syllabus
syllogism
sylph

sylvan
symbol
symmetrical
symmetry
sympathy
symphonic
symphony
symposium
symptom
symptomatic
synagogue
synapse
synchronicity
synchronize
synchronous
syncopation
syndicate
syndrome
synergism
synergy
synethesia
synod
synonym
synonymous
synopsis
syntax
syntheses
synthesis
synthetic
syphilis
syphilitic
syringe
syrup
system
systematic
Szechwan
tabernacle

tableau

taboo

taboos

tabulate

tachometer

tacit

taciturn

tackier

tackiest

tackle

tact

tactics

tae kwan do

taffeta

Tahitian

tailor

Taiwan

Taj Mahal

takeover

talisman

talk

tam-o'-shanter

tamale

tambourine

tampon

tandem

tangelo

tangelos

tangerine

tangible

tangle

tantalize

tantamount

Taoism

tapestries

tapestry

tapioca

tarantella

tarantula

tardier

tardiest

tardiness

tardy

tariff

tarmac

tarnish

tarot

tarpaulin

tarragon

tartar

Tasmanian

tassel

tattle

tattoo

tattoos

taupe

Taurus

taut

tautology

tawdrier

tawdriest

tawdry

tax-deductible

taxonomy

Tchaikovsky

teachability

teachable

teal

tearful

technical

technician

technique

tedious

teenybopper

teepee	tequila
teetotaler	teriyaki
telegenic	termagant
telekinesis	terminal
telephone	termite
TelePrompTer	terra cotta
telethon	terrain
televise	terrarium
temerity	terrestrial
tempera	terrible
temperament	terrier
temperance	terrific
temperate	terrify
temperature	terrifying
tempest	territorial
tempestuous	territories
tempo	terse
temporal	tertiary
temporarily	testify
temporary	testosterone
temporize	testy
temptable	tetanus
temptation	tête-à-tête
tenable	tetracycline
tenacious	Tetrazzini
tenant	Teuton
tendency	textbook
tendentious	texture
tendon	Thailand
tendril	thallium
tenet	than
tension	theater
tentacle	their
tentative	theism
tenuous	theme
tenure	then
tepid	theologian

theology
theorem
theorize
theory
therapeutic
there
therefore
thermometer
thermonuclear
thesaurus
thesis
they're
thiamine
thief
thievery
thieves
thingamabob
thingamajig
thirsty
thirtieth
thistle
Thoreau
thorough
thoroughfare
though
thousand
threshold
threw
thrifty
throng
throttle
through
throughway
thumb
thunderous
thwart
thyme

thyroid
tiara
tibia
tic
ticketed
ticketing
tickle
tiddlywinks
tidier
tidiest
tied
tie-dye
tie-dyed
tie-dyeing
tier
tiered
timbre
timelier
timeliest
timely
timepiece
timorous
timpani
tincture
tine
tingeing
tingle
tinier
tiniest
tinniest
tinsel
tint
tirade
tissue
titanic
titanium
tithe

tithing	tormentor
titillate	tornado
title	tornadoes
tobacco	torpedo
tobacconist	torpedoes
tobaccos	torpid
toboggan	torpor
tofu	torque
toga	tort
together	torte
toil	tortellini
toilet	tortilla
toilette	tortoise
Tokyo	tortoiseshell
tolerance	tortuous
tolerant	totaled
tolled	totaling
tolling	totem
tomato	tottering
tomatoes	touch-tone
tomb	touchable
tombstone	toupee
tome	toupeed
tomorrow	tour
tongue	tourmaline
tongue-tied	tourniquet
tonsil	tousle
tonsillectomy	tout
tonsillitis	toward
tonsorial	towel
too	toweled
tooth	toweling
toothpaste	traceability
topaz	traceable
topic	trachea
topple	tracheotomy
toreador	traditionally

traffic
trafficked
trafficker
trafficking
tragedy
tragicomedy
tragicomic
traipse
traitorous
trajectory
trammel
trample
trampoline
tranquil
tranquilize
tranquilizer
tranquillity
transceiver
transcend
transcendent
transcendental
transfer
transferable
transferring
transient
transistor
transition
transitory
translucent
transmittance
transmitting
transmogrify
transom
transsexual
transship
transubstantiation
transvestite

transvestitism
trapeze
trapezoid
trauma
travail
traveling
travelogue
treacherous
treachery
treacle
treason
treasurer
treasury
treatise
treble
Treblinka
trellis
tremble
tremendous
tremolo
tremulous
trepidation
trespass
trespassed
trespasses
trespassing
tress
tresses
trestle
triangles
Triassic
tribune
tributary
triceps
triceratops
trickle
tricot

tricycle	tsunami
tries	tuber
trifle	tubercle
trifled	tubercular
trifocal	tuberculoid
trim	tuberculosis
trimester	Tucson
tripe	Tuesday
triphthong	tulip
triplicate	tulle
triptych	tumescent
triumph	tumult
trivial	tumultuous
trivially	tunable
trochaic	tundra
trochee	tungsten
trompe l'oeil	turbid
trophies	tureen
troposphere	turgid
troubadour	turnpike
trouble	turpentine
trough	turquoise
troupe	turtle
trousseau	Tutankhamen
truant	tutelage
truculent	tutti-frutti
truffles	tuxedo
truly	TV
trumpery	twelfth
trumpeting	twentieth
truncate	twilight
truncheon	twinging
trundle	twinkle
tryst	two
tsetse fly	tycoon
T-shirt	tying
T-square	type

typesetting
typewriter
typhoid
typhoon
typhus
tyrannical
Tyrannosaurus Rex
tyrant
tyro
ubiquitous
ugliest
ukulele
ulcer
ulcerous
ulterior
ultimate
ultimately
ultimatum
ultrasaurus
ultrasound
umbilical
umbrage
umbrella
umlaut
unacceptable
unanimous
unattended
unavoidable
unawares
unbearable
unbosom
unbowed
uncertain
unchristian
uncircumcised
uncle
unconditional

unconscionable
unconscious
uncontrollable
uncouth
unctuous
undeceive
undeniable
underlying
underprivileged
undesirable
undoubtedly
undue
unduly
unequaled
unequivocal
unerring
unfavorable
unforgettable
unfortunately
unfriendly
ungodly
ungrateful
unguent
unicyclist
uniform
unify
unilateral
uninhabitable
uninterrupted
unique
uniquely
unison
Unitarian
unity
unkempt
unknowable
unmistakable

unnecessary
unpleasant
unpopular
unprecedented
unpretentious
unpronounceable
unremitting
unscrupulous
unsociable
untenable
until
untoward
unwieldy
up-and-coming
upbraid
upheaval
upholstery
uproarious
upside
upstage
uranium
urbane
ureter
urethra
urine
usable
useful
usherette
usually
usurious
usurp
usury
utensil
uterus
uvula
uxoricide
vaccinate

vaccination
vacillate
vacuity
vacuous
vacuum
vague
vain
vain
valedictorian
valedictory
Valentine
valet
Valhalla
valiant
valid
valise
Valium
valorous
valuable
vamoose
vampire
Van Gogh
vandal
vanilla
vanity
vapid
vaporous
variable
varicose
varied
variegated
variety
various
varying
vase
vasectomy
vassal

Vatican	verbally
vaudeville	verbiage
vector	verdigris
vegan	verifiable
vegetable	verily
vegetarian	verisimilitude
vegetative	veritable
vehement	verity
vehicle	vermicelli
vehicular	vermilion
veil	vermin
vein	vermouth
Velcro	vernacular
veldt	versatile
velocity	versatility
velour	versify
venal	version
veneer	versus
venerable	vertebrae
venereal	vertebrate
venetian	vertigo
Venetian	verve
Venezuela	vessels
vengeful	vestibule
venial	vestige
Venice	vestigial
venison	vetch
venom	veteran
venomous	veterinarian
venous	veterinary
ventilate	veto
ventilation	vetoes
ventricle	vex
ventriloquism	vexatious
ventriloquist	viability
venue	viable
veracious	vial

viand
vibrato
vicarious
vice
vice versa
vichyssoise
vicinity
vicious
vicissitudes
victim
victual
victuals
vigilance
vigilant
vigilante
vignette
vigorous
vilify
villain
vim
vinaigrette
vindictive
vinegar
vineyard
vintage
vintner
vinyl
violet
violin
virtually
virtue
virtuosity
virtuoso
virtuous
virulence
virulent
visage

vis-à-vis
visceral
viscid
viscosity
viscount
viscous
visibility
visible
visualize
vitally
vitamin
vitiate
vitriol
vivacious
Vivaldi
vivid
vivify
vivisection
vizier
vocabulary
vociferous
vodka
vogue
voice
voilà
volatile
volatility
volcano
volcanoes
volition
Voltaire
voltmeter
voluble
volume
voluminous
voluntarism
voluntary

volunteer
voluptuary
voluptuous
vomiting
voodoo
voracious
vortex
vouchsafe
vox populi
voyager
voyageur
voyeur
vs.
vulgar
vulgarize
Vulgate
vulnerable
vulture
wafer
waif
wainscot
wainscoting
waiver
walkie talkie
walkway
wallet
walleye
wallop
walloping
wall-to-wall
wan
wanderlust
wane
wangle
warble
warehouse
warm-blooded

warm-hearted
warrant
warranty
warrior
wary
wash-and-wear
wassail
wastrel
waterborne
waterlog
water-resistant
watershed
water-ski
Watusi
waver
waxen
wayfarer
wayfaring
wealth
wean
weapon
wearable
weariness
wearisome
weary
weather
Wednesday
weevil
weft
weigh
weight
Weimaraner
weird
welcome
welfare
well-being
well-known

well-to-do
welsh
Welsh
welterweight
wench
werewolf
whacky
wheedle
wheel
wheeler-dealer
whence
whenever
whereabouts
whereas
wheresoever
whereupon
wherever
wherewithal
whet
whether
whetstone
whey
Whig
whimsical
whimsy
whine
whippet
whippoorwill
whir
whirligig
whirring
whiskey
whisper
whistle
whistlestop
whither
whittle

whoever
wholesale
wholesome
wholly
whomever
whooping cough
whore
whorl
who's
whose
widely
width
wield
Wiener schnitzel
wildebeest
wile
will-o'-the-wisp
willful
willy-nilly
wily
wince
windjammer
windward
Winnebago
winnow
winsome
wintry
wiretap
wiretapping
Wisconsin
wiseacre
wisecrack
wishy-washy
wisteria
witch hazel
witch-hunt
withal

withdrawal
wither
withered
withhold
without
withstood
witticism
wizard
wizened
wobble
woebegone
woeful
wok
wolfsbane
wolverine
wolves
womb
wombat
women
won ton
wondrous
wont
won't
woolen
woolly
Worcestershire
workable
work force
world-weariness
worldwide
worriment
worrywart
worshipful
worsted
worthwhile
would-be
wrack

wraith
wrangle
wrath
wreath
wreathe
wreck
wren
wrest
wrestler
wretched
wriggle
wrinkle
wrist
writ
writhe
writing
written
wrong
wrought
wry
wrier
wunderkind
wurst
X-rated
x-ray
x-rayed
Xavier
xebec
xenophobe
xenophobic
xerography
Xerox
xylan
xylem
xylophone
yacht
Yahweh

yak
yang
Yankee
yarmulke
year-round
yearned
Yemen
yen
yenta
yeoman
yesteryear
yew
Yiddish
yield
yielding
yin
yippie
yodel
yogi
yogurt
yoke
yokel
yolk
Yom Kippur
yore
you're
youngster
your
yucca

Yuletide
zany
zeal
zealot
zealous
Zeitgeist
zenith
zephyr
zeppelin
zestful
Zeus
zigzag
zilch
Zimbabwe
zinc
zinnia
zircon
zither
ziti
zodiac
zombie
zoological
zoology
zucchini
zulu
Zurich
zwieback
zygote

The Words You Should Know How To Spell: Geographical/Astronomical Supplement

U.S. States and Cities

The following state-by-state breakdown contains two categories of place names: capitals and other major cities within a state, included regardless of the difficulty of the spelling, and towns with potentially troublesome spellings over about 10,000 population. For information on the spellings of the names of smaller towns, you may find an atlas or detailed dictionary helpful.

ALABAMA
Anniston
Auburn
Birmingham
Cullman
Decatur
Dothan
Gadsden
Mobile
Opelika
Phenix City
Scottsboro
Sylacauga
Talladega
Tuscaloosa
Vestavia Hills

ALASKA
Anchorage
Barrow
Fairbanks
Juneau
Ketchikan
Valdez

ARIZONA
Ajo
Mesa
Nogales
Phoenix
Scottsdale
Tucson
Yuma

ARKANSAS
Blytheville
Fayetteville
Little Rock
Texarkana

CALIFORNIA
Alameda
Altadena
Azusa
Berkeley
Big Sur
Brea
Burlingame
Calabasas
Calexico
Calistoga

Camarillo
Carlsbad
Carpinteria
Cerritos
Chico
Cucamonga
Cupertino
Daly City
El Cajon
El Cerrito
El Monte
El Segundo
Escondido
Eureka
Fresno
Goleta
Hemet
Hillsborough
Inglewood
Inverness
Lafayette
La Mesa
Livermore
Lodi
Los Angeles
Lompoc
Lynwood
Malibu
Martinez
Mendocino
Menlo Park
Merced
Millbrae
Milpitas
Mission Viejo
Modesto
Novato
Ojai
Pasadena
Petaluma
Pittsburg
Rancho Cordova
Rancho Palos
   Verdes
Sacramento
Salinas
San Diego
San Francisco
San Mateo

Santa Cruz
Santee
Sausalito
Sunnyvale
Vallejo
Visalia
Whittier
Yreka
Yuba City

COLORADO
Arvada
Aurora
Boulder
Denver
Englewood
Greeley
Littleton
Northglenn
Pueblo
Westminster

CONNECTICUT
Ansonia
Bridgeport
Danbury
Glastonbury
Greenwich
Hartford
Meriden
Milford
Norwalk
Shelton
Stamford
Waterbury
Willimantic
Windsor Locks

DELAWARE
Dover
Newark
Wilmington

DISTRICT OF
   COLUMBIA
District of
   Columbia

FLORIDA
Altamonte
   Springs
Bartow
Belle Glade
Boca Raton
Boynton Beach
Bradenton
Carol City
Cocoa Beach
Fort Lauderdale
Gainesville
Hallandale
Hialeah
Immokalee
Jacksonville
Lauderdale Lakes
Lake Magdalene
Leisure City
Margate
Melbourne
Merritt Island
Miami
Miramar
New Smyrna
   Beach
Orlando
Ormond Beach
Palm Beach
Pensacola
Pinellas Park
Pompano Beach
Port Charlotte
Riviera Beach
St. Petersburg
Sarasota
Tallahassee
Tamarac
West Palm Beach

GEORGIA
Albany
Athens
Atlanta
Augusta
Belvedere Park
Brunswick
Columbus
Decatur

La Grange
Mableton
Macon
Marietta
Savannah
Smyrna
Thomasville
Valdosta
Vidalia
Warner Robins
Waycross

HAWAII
Aiea
Ewa Beach
Hilo
Honolulu
Kailua
Kaneohe
Mililani Town
Wahiawa
Waipahu

IDAHO
Boise
Coeur d'Alene
Idaho Falls
Lewiston
Moscow
Nampa
Pocatello

ILLINOIS
Addison
Alsip
Alton
Aurora
Belleville
Belvidere
Bensenville
Berwyn
Bloomington
Bolingbrook
Bourbonnais
Carpentersville
Centralia
Champaign
Charleston

Chicago
Chillicothe
Cicero
Creve Couer
Danville
Decatur
De Kalb
Des Plaines
Downers Grove
Elgin
Evanston
Galesburg
Glendale Heights
Glen Ellyn
Glenview
Highland Park
Jacksonville
Joliet
Kankakee
Lansing
Loves Park
Maywood
Melrose Park
Midlothian
Moline
Mundelein
Naperville
Niles
O'Fallon
Ottawa
Palatine
Pekin
Peoria
Rantoul
Romeoville
Sauk Village
Schaumburg
Schiller Park
Skokie
Springfield
Tinley Park
Urbana
Villa Park
Waukegan
Wilmette
Winnetka
Zion

INDIANA
Anderson
Beech Grove
Bloomington
Carmel
Columbus
Elkhart
Evansville
Fort Wayne
Gary
Goshen
Highland
Indianapolis
Kokomo
Lafayette
Marion
Merrillville
Muncie
New Albany
New Castle
Portage
Richmond
South Bend
Terre Haute
Valparaiso
Vincennes
Wabash

IOWA
Ankeny
Bettendorf
Council Bluffs
Davenport
Des Moines
Dubuque
Keokuk
Marion
Muscatine
Oskaloosa
Ottumwa
Sioux City
Urbandale
Waterloo

KANSAS
Arkansas City
Chanute
Coffeyville

133

El Dorado
Emporia
Hays
Hutchinson
Kansas City
Lawrence
Leavenworth
Leawood
Olathe
Ottawa
Pittsburg
Salina
Shawnee
Topeka
Wichita

KENTUCKY
Bowling Green
Erlanger
Florence
Frankfort
Highview
Jeffersontown
Lexington
Louisville
Madisonville
Middlesboro
Okolona
Owensboro
Paducah
St. Matthews
Somerset

LOUISIANA
Abbeville
Alexandria
Bastrop
Baton Rouge
Bayou Cane
Bogalusa
Bossier City
Chalmette
De Ridder
Eunice
Gretna
Houma
Lafayette
La Place
Marrero

Metairie
New Orleans
Opelousas
Shreveport
Sulphur
Tallulah
Thibodaux

MAINE
Auburn
Augusta
Bangor
Biddeford
Kennebunkport
Portland
Presque Isle
Saco

MARYLAND
Aberdeen
Annapolis
Baltimore
Bethesda
Bowie
Chillum
Dundalk
Gaithersburg
Joppa
Lutherville-
    Timonium
Potomac
Randallstown
Salisbury
Severn
Severna Park
Suitland

MASSACHUSETTS
Abington
Athol
Attleboro
Auburn
Boston
Chelsea
Chicopee
Cohasset
Falmouth
Gloucester
Holliston

Holyoke
Lawrence
Leicester
Leominster
Marlborough
Methuen
Middleboro
Newburyport
Northampton
Peabody
Pittsfield
Saugus
Scituate
Seekonk
Shrewsbury
Somerville
Southborough
Swansea
Taunton
Tewksbury
Wellesley
Westborough
Weymouth
Worcester
Yarmouth

MICHIGAN
Adrian
Albion
Allen Park
Ann Arbor
Bangor Township
Beecher
Berkley
Clawson
Dearborn
Dearborn Heights
Detroit
Escanaba
Grosse Pointe
Grosse Pointe
    Woods
Grosse Pointe
    Park
Kalamazoo
Lansing
Livonia
Madison Heights
Marquette

Menominee
Muskegon
Muskegon
  Heights
Owosso
River Rouge
Romulus
St. Clair Shores
Sault Ste. Marie
Wyandotte
Ypsilanti

MINNESOTA
Albert Lea
Anoka
Bemidji
Brainerd
Cloquet
Columbia Heights
Duluth
Eagan
Eden Prairie
Edina
Faribault
Fergus Falls
Inner Grove
  Heights
Mankato
Minneapolis
Minnetonka
Moorhead
Mounds View
Owatonna
Ramsey
Red Wing
Robbinsdale
St. Paul
Shakopee
Stillwater
Winona
Woodbury

MISSISSIPPI
Biloxi
Columbus
Corinth
Hattiesburg
Jackson

McComb
Meridian
Moss Point
Natchez
Pascagoula
Picayune ·
Southaven
Tupelo
Yazoo City

MISSOURI
Affton
Ballwin
Bellefontaine
  Neighbors
Berkeley
Bridgeton
Cape Girardeau
Carthage
Columbia
Creve Coeur
Excelsior Springs
Ferguson
Hannibal
Jefferson City
Kansas City
Kennett
Lees Summit
Lemay
Marshall
Moberly
Poplar Bluff
Richmond
  Heights
Rolla
St. Louis
Sedalia
Sikeston

MONTANA
Anaconda
Bozeman
Butte
Helena
Kalispell
Missoula
Sidney

NEBRASKA
Beatrice
Bellevue
Columbus
Kearney
Lincoln
Norfolk
North Platte
Omaha
Scottsbluff
South Sioux City

NEVADA
Carson City
Elko
Fallon
Las Vegas
Reno
Winnemucca

NEW
  HAMPSHIRE
Concord
Derry
Dover
Exeter
Goffstown
Hooksett
Keene
Manchester
Marlborough
Nashua

NEW JERSEY
Asbury Park
Avenel
Belleville
Bellmawr
Berkeley Heights
Bridgeton
Brigantine
Browns Mills
Carteret
Cinnaminson
Collingswood
Colonia
Delran
Englewood

135

Ewing Township
Fair Lawn
Glassboro
Gloucester City
Hackensack
Hackettstown
Hammonton
Harrison
Hasbrouck
  Heights
Iselin
Kearny
Kenilworth
Kinnelon
Lindenwold
Lyndhurst
Mahwah
Matawan
Montclair
Moorestown
Morristown
Newark
Nutley
Palisades Park
Paramus
Parsippany
Passaic
Paterson
Pennsauken
Pequannock
Phillipsburg
Piscataway
Plainsboro
Rahway
Ramsey
Ridgefield
Roselle
Sayreville
Secaucus
Somers Point
Summit
Trenton
Wanaque
Weehawken
West Paterson
Willingboro
Woodbury
Wyckoff

NEW MEXICO
Albuquerque
Armijo
Artesia
Carlsbad
Deming
Gallup
Hobbs
Las Cruces
Los Alamos
Lovington
Portales
Roswell
Santa Fe

NEW YORK
Albany
Auburn
Batavia
Bellmore
Bethpage
Binghamton
Bronx
Brooklyn
Canandaigua
Centereach
Cheektowaga
Cohoes
Copiague
Depew
Dobbs Ferry
Elmira
Glens Falls
Greenwich Village
Harrison
Hartsdale
Hauppauge
Irondequoit
Islip
Ithaca
Jericho
Lackawanna
Levittown
Mamaroneck
Manhattan
Massapequa
Massena
Mineola
Monsey

Nesconset
Newburgh
New York
Niagara Falls
Niskayuna
Ogdensburg
Oneida
Oneonta
Ossining
Oswego
Patchogue
Queens
Peekskill
Plattsburgh
Poughkeepsie
Ridgemont
Schenectady
Staten Island
Syracuse
Tonawanda
Utica
Wantagh
Watervliet
Westbury
White Plains
Woodmere

NORTH
  CAROLINA
Albemarle
Asheville
Boone
Cary
Charlotte
Durham
Fayetteville
Gastonia
Greensboro
Kannapolis
Kinston
Lenoir
New Bern
Raleigh
Reidsville
Roanoake Rapids
Salisbury
Winston-Salem

NORTH DAKOTA
Bismarck
Dickinson
Minot
Williston

OHIO
Ashtabula
Barberton
Beavercreek
Bedford Heights
Bexley
Bowling Green
Brooklyn
Brunswick
Bucyrus
Chillicothe
Cincinnati
Columbus
Coshocton
Cuyahoga Falls
Elyria
Gahanna
Garfield Heights
Huber Heights
Ironton
Kettering
Lima
Lorain
Lyndhurst
Madeira
Maumee
Monfort Heights
Newark
Painesville
Piqua
Ravenna
Reynoldsburg
Richmond Heights
Sandusky
Sheffield Lake
Sidney
Solon
Steubenville
Sylvania
Tallmadge
Vermilion

Wapakoneta
Wickliffe
Willoughby
Wooster
Xenia
Zanesville

OKLHOMA
Ada
Altus
Chickasha
Claremore
Edmond
Enid
McAlester
Muskogee
Oklahoma City
Okmulgee
Ponca City
Sapulpa
Shawnee
Tulsa

OREGON
Aloha
Coos Bay
Eugene
Grants Pass
Gresham
Hillsboro
Keizer
Lake Oswego
Milwaukie
Newberg
Portland
Salem
The Dalles
Tigard
West Linn

PENNSYLVANIA
Aliquippa
Allentown
Altoona
Ardmore
Bellevue
Bensalem
Berwick
Bloomsburg

Broomall
Bryn Mawr
Canonsburg
Chambersburg
Clairton
Coatesville
Columbia
Connellsville
Conshohocken
Croydon
Dormont
Duquesne
Emmaus
Erie
Fairless Hill
Greensburg
Harrisburg
Hazleton
Hermitage
Huntingdon Valley
Jeannette
Lancaster
Lansdowne
Levittown
Lower Burrell
McCandless
McKeesport
Millcreek
Monessen
Murrysville
Natrona Heights
New Castle
North Versailles
Philadelphia
Pittsburgh
Roslyn
Shamokin
Stowe Township
Sunbury
Upper St. Clair
West Chester
West Mifflin
West Norriton
Wilkes-Barre
Wilkinsburg
Yeadon

RHODE ISLAND
Berkeley
Coventry
Pawtucket
Providence
Warwick

SOUTH CAROLINA
Aiken
Cayce
Charleston
Columbia
Easley
Gaffney
Hanahan
Laurens
Myrtle Beach
Sumter
Taylors
Walterboro

SOUTH DAKOTA
Aberdeen
Pierre
Sioux Falls
Vermillion
Yankton

TENNESSEE
Bartlett
Chattanooga
Columbia
Cookeville
Dyersburg
Elizabethton
Gallatin
Greeneville
Humboldt
Knoxville
McMinnville
Memphis
Morristown
Nashville
Tullahoma

TEXAS
Abilene
Amarillo
Austin
Beaumont
Burleson
Carrollton
Cleburne
Corpus Christi
Corsicana
Dallas
Del Rio
Denison
De Soto
Dumas
El Paso
Farmers Branch
Fort Worth
Friendswood
Gainesville
Grand Prairie
Haltom City
Harlingen
Hereford
Houston
Kerrville
Kilgore
Killeen
La Marque
Lamesa
Laredo
League City
Levelland
Lubbock
McAllen
McKinney
Marshall
Mesquite
Nacogdoches
Nederland
Odessa
Pearland
Pecos
Pharr
Plano
Port Lavaca
Robstown
Rosenberg
San Antonio
San Benito
San Marcos

Seguin
Stephenville
Sulphur Springs
Sweetwater
Texarkana
Uvalde
Waco
Watauga
Waxahachie
Wichita Falls

UTAH
Cottonwood
   Heights
Holladay
Kearns
Midvale
Murray
Ogden
Orem
Provo
Salt Lake City
Taylorsville
Tooele

VERMONT
Bennington
Burlington
Montpelier
Rutland
St. Johnsbury

VIRGINIA
Alexandria
Annandale
Baileys
   Crossroads
Blacksburg
Bon Air
Bristol
Charlottesville
Chesapeake
Christianburg
Colonial Heights
Engleside
Falls Church
Harrisonburg
Hybla Valley
Leesburg

Lynchburg
McLean
Manassas
Mechanicsville
Newport News
Norfolk
Petersburg
Poquoson
Portsmouth
Pulaski
Richmond
Roanoake
Staunton
Suffolk
Vienna
Wytheville

WASHINGTON
Aberdeen
Anacortes
Auburn
Bellevue
Bellingham
Bremerton
Burien
Centralia
Edmonds
Everett
Kelso
Kennewick
Lacey
Lynnwood
Mercer Island
Moses Lake
Olympia

Pasco
Port Angeles
Puyallup
Redmond
Renton
Riverton Heights
Seattle
Spokane
Tacoma
Vancouver
Walla Walla
Wenatchee
Yakima

WEST VIRGINIA
Beckley
Charleston
Clarksburg
Martinsburg
Parkersburg
St. Albans
Vienna
Weirton
Wheeling

WISCONSIN
Allouez
Ashwaubenon
Baraboo
Beloit
Cedarburg
Chippewa Falls
Cudahy
De Pere
Eau Claire

Fond du Lac
Kenosha
La Crosse
Madison
Manitowoc
Menasha
Menomonee Falls
Menomonie
Mequon
Merrill
Milwaukee
Muskego
Neenah
Oconomowoc
Onalaska
Oshkosh
Platteville
Racine
Sheboygan
Stevens Point
Sun Prairie
Waukesha
Wausau
Wauwatosa

WYOMING
Casper
Cheyenne
Gillette
Laramie
Worland

Foreign Countries

Afghanistan
Albania
Algeria
Andorra
Angola
Antigua and
    Barbuda
Argentina
Armenia
Australia

Austria
Azerbaijan
Bahamas
Bahrain
Bangladesh
Barbados
Belarus
Belgium
Belize
Benin

Bhutan
Bolivia
Bosnia and
    Hercegovina
Botswana
Brazil
Brunei
    Darussalam
Bulgaria
Burkina Faso

Burundi
Cambodia
Cameroon
Canada
Cape Verde
Central African
     Republic
Chad
Chile
China
Colombia
Comoros
Congo
Costa Rica
Côte d'Ivoire
Croatia
Cuba
Cyprus
Czech Republic
Denmark
Djibouti
Dominica
Dominican
     Republic
Ecuador
Egypt
El Salvador
Equatorial Guinea
Eritrea
Estonia
Ethiopia
Fiji
Finland
France
Gabon
Gambia
Georgia
Germany
Ghana
Greece
Grenada
Guatemala
Guinea
Guinea-Bissau
Guyana
Haiti
Honduras
Hungary
Iceland

India
Indonesia
Iran
Iraq
Ireland
Israel
Italy
Jamaica
Japan
Kazakhstan
Kenya
Korea, North
Korea, South
Kuwait
Kyrgyzstan
Laos
Latvia
Lebanon
Lesotho
Liberia
Libya
Liechtenstein
Lithuania
Luxembourg
Macedonia (The
     Former
     Yugoslav
     Republic of
     Macedonia)
Madagascar
Malawi
Malaysia
Maldives
Mali
Malta
Marshall Islands
Mauritania
Mauritius
Mexico
Micronesia
Moldova
Monaco
Mongolia
Morocco
Mozambique
Myanmar
Namibia
Nepal
Netherlands

New Zealand
Nicaragua
Niger
Nigeria
Norway
Oman
Pakistan
Panama
Papua New
     Guinea
Paraguay
Peru
Philippines
Poland
Portugal
Qatar
Romania
Russian
     Federation
Rwanda
St. Kitts and
     Nevis
St. Lucia
St. Vincent and
     the Grenadines
San Marino
Sao Tome and
     Principe
Saudi Arabia
Senegal
Serbia
Seychelles
Sierra Leone
Singapore
Slovak Republic
Slovenia
Solomon Islands
Somalia
South Africa
Spain
Sri Lanka
Sudan
Suriname
Swaziland
Sweden
Syria
Tajikistan
Tanzania
Thailand

Togo
Trinidad and
   Tobago
Tunisia
Turkey
Turkmenistan
Uganda
Ukraine

United Arab
   Emirates
United Kingdom
Uruguay
Uzbekistan
Vanuatu
Venezuela
Vietnam

Western Samoa
Yemen, Republic
   of
Yugoslavia
Zaire
Zambia
Zimbabwe

Major Foreign Cities

Addis Ababa,
   Ethiopia
Alexandria, Egypt
Algiers, Algeria
Amsterdam,
   Netherlands
Antwerp,
   Belgium
Athens, Greece
Baghdad, Iraq
Bangkok,
   Thailand
Barcelona, Spain
Barranquilla,
   Colombia
Beijing, China
Beirut, Lebanon
Belo Horizonte,
   Brazil
Berlin, Germany
Bilbao, Spain
Birmingham,
   England
Bogota, Colombia
Bombay, India
Brasilia, Brasil
Brisbane,
   Australia
Brussels, Belgium
Bucharest,
   Romania
Budapest,
   Hungary
Buenos Aires,
   Argentina
Bytom, Poland
Cairo, Egypt

Calcutta, India
Cali, Colombia
Cape Town,
   South Africa
Caracas,
   Venezuela
Casablanca,
   Morocco
Chelyabinsk,
   Russian
   Federation
Chongqing, China
Cologne,
   Germany
Copenhagen,
   Denmark
Cordoba,
   Argentina
Curitiba, Brazil
Delhi, India
Dhaka,
   Bangladesh
Dublin, Ireland
Durban, South
   Africa
Dusseldorf,
   Germany
Fortaleza, Brazil
Frankfurt *am
   Main*, Germany
Glasgow, Scotland
Glwice, Poland
Guadalajara,
   Mexico
Guayaquil,
   Ecuador

Hamburg,
   Germany
Hanover,
   Germany
Havana, Cuba
Islamabad,
   Pakistan
Istanbul, Turkey
Jakarta, Indonesia
Johannesburg,
   South Africa
Karachi, Pakistan
Katowice, Poland
Khartoum, Sudan
Kinshasa, Zaire
Kobe, Japan
Kuala Lumpur,
   Malaysia
Kuwait, Kuwait
Kyoto, Japan
Lagos, Nigeria
Leeds-Bradford,
   England
Lille, France
Lima, Peru
Liverpool,
   England
Lodz, Poland
London, England
Lyons, France
Madras, India
Madrid, Spain
Manila, The
   Philippines
Mannheim,
   Germany
Marseille, France

141

Medellin, Colombia
Melbourne, Australia
Mexico City, Mexico
Milan, Italy
Montevideo, Uruguay
Montreal, Canada
Moscow, Russian Federation
Munich, Germany
New Delhi, India
Newcastle-Sunderland, England
Novosibirsk, Russian Federation
Nuremberg, Germany
Opporto, Portugal
Osaka, Japan
Ottawa, Canada
Paris, France
Porto Alegre, Brazil
Prague, Czech Republic
Pyongyang, North Korea
Rangoon, Burma
Recife, Brazil
Rio De Janeiro, Brazil
Rome, Italy
Rosario, Argentina
Salvador, Brazil
Santiago, Chile
Santo Domingo, Dominican Republic
Sao Paulo, Brazil
Sapporo, Japan
Seoul, South Korea
Shanghai, China
Shenyang, China
Smolensk, Russian Federation
Sofia, Bulgaria
Stockholm, Sweden
Stuttgart, Germany
St. Petersburg, Russian Federation
Sydney, Australia
Taipei, Taiwan
Tbilisi, Georgia
Tehran, Iran
Tel Aviv, Israel
The Ruhr (Essen-Dortmund-Duisburg), Germany
Tokyo, Japan
Toronto, Canada
Tunis, Tunisia
Turin, Italy
Valencia, Spain
Vancouver, Canada
Vienna, Austria
Winnipeg, Canada
Wuhan, China
Yokohama, Japan

The Planets of the Solar System and Their Moons

Earth
The Moon

Jupiter
(Largest moons:)
Amalthea
Callisto
Europa
Ganymede
Io

Mars
Deimos
Phobos

Mercury
(No moons.)

Neptune
Despina
Galatea
Larissa
Naiad
Nereid
Proteus
Thalassa
Triton

Pluto
Charon

Saturn
(Largest moons:)
Dione
Enceladus
Hyperion
Iapetus
Mimas
Pan
Phoebe
Rhea
Tethys
Titan

Uranus
Ariel
Belinda
Bianca
Cordelia
Cressida
Desdemona

Juliet
Miranda
Oberon
Ophelia
Portia
Rosalind
Puck

Titania
Umbriel

Venus
(No moons.)

Major Stars

Achernar
Aldebaran
Alpha Centauri
Alpha-one Crucis
Altair
Antares
Arcturus
Bellatrix
Beta Centauri
Beta Crucis
Betelgeuse
Canopus

Capella
Castor
Deneb
Epsilon Canis
  Majoris
Epsilon Carinae
Epsilon Ursae
  Majoris
Eta Carinae
Fomalhaut
Gamma Crucis
Lambda Scorpii

Mira
Pollux
Procyon
Regulus
Rigel
Sirius
Spica
Vega

EAST LONDON
SUFFRAGETTES